sacred
baby names

kjirstin youngberg

PLAIN SIGHT PUBLISHING
AN IMPRINT OF CEDAR FORT, INC.
SPRINGVILLE, UTAH

This is not an official publication of The Church of Jesus Christ of Latter-day Saints. The opinions and views expressed herein belong solely to the author and do not necessarily represent the opinions or views of Cedar Fort, Inc. Permission for the use of sources, graphics, and photos is also solely the responsibility of the author.

ISBN 13: 978-1-4621-1024-7

Published by Plain Sight Publishing, an imprint of Cedar Fort, Inc.
2373 W. 700 S., Springville, UT 84663
Distributed by Cedar Fort, Inc., www.cedarfort.com

LIBRARY OF CONGRESS CATALOGING-IN-PUBLICATION DATA

Youngberg, Kjirstin, 1953- author.
Sacred baby names / Kjirstin Youngberg.
pages cm
Includes bibliographical references and index.
ISBN 978-1-4621-1024-7 (alk. paper)
1. Names, Personal--Religious aspects--Dictionaries. 2. Names, Personal--Dictionaries--English.
I. Title.

CS2377.Y68 2012
929.4'4--dc23

2012015543

Cover design by Angela D. Olsen
Cover design © 2012 by Lyle Mortimer
Edited and typeset by Emily S. Chambers

Printed in the United States of America

10 9 8 7 6 5 4 3 2 1

Printed on acid-free paper

To Rachel and JD Payne, who may need this in
the not-too-distant future,

Thanks to Arslan Baig, Jessica Nicole Whitby, and
Christopher Taney for their exceptional assistance
in my research.

introduction

A T THE MOMENT OF BIRTH, EVEN THE MOST ARDENT OF ATHEISTS recognizes, if only for an instant, something truly divine in the creation of a newborn baby so innocent and pure, that the event can only be proclaimed as sacred.

In the beginning, God was so protective of His own name that He would not speak it nor permit anyone else to even know it. When Moses asked, "God said unto Moses, I Am That I Am: and He said, Thus shalt thou say unto the children of Israel, I Am hath sent me unto you" (Exodus 3:14).

Even before man first came to dwell upon the earth, names served an important function to our heavenly parents. Jeremiah, John the Baptist, and Jesus all received names before they were born. As titles of power or station, names were subject to change as callings changed. Simon, a fisherman, became Peter when he was called to be an Apostle. Michael, the archangel, was called Adam, which means "man," when he left his heavenly sphere to accept his assigned role as the first man in Eden. His helpmeet was one day to become the mother of everything living, so he named her Eve, which in Hebrew means "life." Adam then went on to name every creature in the ocean, sky, and earth. Names are significant. Our names are essential.

Jesus is the name of the Savior, spelled as in the original Greek, though Aramaic in origin. Its Hebrew equivalent is *Yehoshua* or *Yeshua* or, as we say in English, Joshua. This name means "Help of Jehovah," or "Savior." Though Joshua is as common a name as Matthew or Jacob today, the name was given divinely to Joseph when the angel said, "And thou shalt call his name Jesus: for he shall save his people from their sins" (Matthew 1:21).

Jehovah is the English version of the Hebrew, *YAHWEH* or *JAHVEH*, signifying "the eternal or self-existent one." It is seen in the Old Testament as "LORD," printed in all capital letters. In Hebrew, it is *EHYEH* or *I AM*, as Moses learned on the mountain. Known as a tetragrammaton, or four letters, the Hebrew *Yod, Hey, Vay,* and *Hey* compose *YHVH*, considered the most holy name ever created.

Broken down, it was a formal title of Messiah: *Yehoshua Ben David* (using Hebrew characters), which then became *Yeshua,* Messiah's everyday name (also using Hebrew characters). The difference between *Yehoshua* and *Yeshua* is like the difference between "Samuel" and "Sam" or "Dan" and "Daniel Ben Judah." The *nomina sacra* ("sacred names")symbols for *Yeshua* in the early times were on papyri. These forms were in the earliest Greek manuscripts. Usually Greek symbols stood for the Hebrew insertion of *Yeshua* into the text. By the fourth century, scribes discarded the *nomina sacra* symbols of the Jerusalem congregation in favor of the Greek. Proper pronunciation was lost and is now said as [ee] [ay] [soo]. Later, a Greek font modernized it to standardize the text. It then became *Iesu* in Late Latin. When it was translated into Latin, the initial "y" sound was still intact, the "sh" was still missing, and the Greek nominative sigma ending was dropped. Then in Old English (*Iesus* or *Yesus*), the influence of Greek sigma ending was restored, but the "sh" and "ayin" were still missing. In Middle English it became *Jesus* (Jee zus.) The original "y" sound was lost due to French influence by the Norman invasion of 1066 and the "waw" sound was also lost. A modern English comparison would be the letter Y versus J, "ee" versus "ay," "z" versus "sh," "uh" versus "oo," and "s" versus "ah."

I don't expect you to want to go into so much detail with your children's names, but you are welcome to do so. Christ is not a name but a sacred title. It is also Greek and means the same thing as its Hebrew equivalent, *Messias,* or *Messiah* meaning "the Anointed One." Other titles have specific meanings. Lord, Mediator, Lamb of God, Son of Man, Son of God, Ruler of Creation, Only Begotten Son, Light of the World, Savior, King of Kings, Lord of Lords, Redeemer, and Emmanuel each have distinct meanings representative of His divinity and Godship.

Stories have always been important to us, no matter where or when we live. The story of Adam and Eve is the same in Jewish, Christian, Buddhist, and Islamic tradition. Oral stories passed down for centuries on obscure island nations and the great myths of northern Europe often bear striking similarities. A creation story with similar themes can be found among every small outpost in every race and culture living today. The names "Adam" and "Eve" are found in most languages, and some of the many variations are included in this book.

We pass on stories to our children, and they see themselves in the characters and learn lessons of value they will use throughout their lives. Even today, mothers with a passion for a certain story will chose to name a child for a character in the story or perhaps the actor who portrayed him on film. A father who remembers a childhood hero with a particular trait may choose to name his baby after him in the hope of passing a noble feature on to his offspring.

Trends toward unusual names or naming a child for a familiar fruit, color, or place name, are becoming common. Children are sometimes subject to teasing because they are too young to stand up to classmates who may taunt them over an unusual name. Keep in mind though that many religious names have withstood the tests of time. Ask any centenarian named Elizabeth or Thomas what they think of their name, and the answer will invariably be something like, "I'm thankful my parents didn't name me 'aeroplane' just because it was popular at the time." Other religious names are more obscure, and thought must be given before bestowing them upon your innocent child.

Many a young mother had a favorite name she gave every doll she ever owned and can't imagine her first real baby would carry any other name. Some first-time fathers have known their firstborn sons would bear their own name followed by a "junior" or herald the III, IV, or even the XVIII in a long line of a name so ancient, every kid on the playground is guaranteed to make fun of him from preschool through junior high. How do you keep a tradition but avoid mockery? What happens when you have another son, or a long line of them, once the first junior has your name? If you continue having children, you must keep finding names for them.

So, like many parents, you've decided to choose religious names to honor your faith. This is great news if your child is a son and you're using the Old Testament. You'll have over three hundred names to choose from with just the first initial *A*. If your offspring is female, and you're using the Book of Mormon, the selection drops to a grand total of six, and three of those names are also found in the Bible. Perhaps this is why so many parents have chosen to stick with Hebrew names, and why others have become creative in the cut-and-paste game of child-naming, grabbing a few letters from one parent and some from the other.

A word about these made-up names. In my research for this book, I interviewed and corresponded with many experts in the field of baby names. One is Don Norton, a retired professor of English from Brigham Young University. Dr. Norton has long held an interest in the use of two-part names and wrote on the use of prefixes La-, Le- (which are both traditional French prefixes, but are overused in some cultures), Ray, Val, Vee, Shir-, Char-, Lee-, and so on (they found some seven hundred of them!), plus any number (four hundred or so) of suffixes, like -von, -ann, -lynn, and so on.

Dr. Norton claimed his personal favorite of all the hundreds of horrific prefix titles was the name "Latrina," which was bestowed upon an innocent baby girl not long ago. Perhaps her parents never had to dig one. "This (naming style) was something of (an) epidemic in rural and small-town western states from about 1890 to recent decades," he said.

A website started by Wes and Cari Clark called "The Utah Baby Namer" is well worth visiting (http://wesclark.com/ubn/). This couple has been collecting unusual baby names for many years. You will laugh if you don't cry over the thought of well-intentioned parents who end up giving children names most often carried by strippers or pharmaceutical medications.

Many studies have determined that our first given names can exclude us from jobs. In several field experiments, Bertrand and Mullainathan (2004) randomly assigned names with different ethnicities (African American or Caucasian) to résumés. They found that résumés with Caucasian-sounding names received 50 percent more response and were considered to be of "higher quality" or "intelligence" based entirely upon the name. It has been pointed out that many of these made-up names sound, as one of my sources said, "like the guy you expect to see with the football but are startled when you discover it's some skinny white girl from Idaho." In September 2006, a show was aired on the ABC television program *20/20* that found similar results. "I think it's great for (my) hiring (practices), since I don't want no blacks or Mormons working for me," one small business employer in California admitted. He obviously had no idea that the researcher he spoke on the phone with was a British-African Mormon whose name, fortunately, was Charles. Prejudices like these are ridiculous, and we may laugh, but we should consider future bias toward our children as we contemplate these invented names.

Some parents have different religious backgrounds, and even if one has converted, they may wish to acknowledge this heritage by naming a baby in honor of it.

Based on texts from Muslim writers and the Qur'an, the Islamic faith includes the ninety-nine Most Beautiful Names of God. You'll never find a Muslim being called with one of these names, as they are considered sacred to Allah. You will see Muslim men being called *abd*, or "servant of" followed by the name, which is most often an attribute, such as the Creator, the Omniscient, or the Forgiver. Muslim women may be called *amat* meaning "female servant of" and then one of those names. This practice is also seen among the Hindus' Brahman, Bahá'í, and other religions. There are, in fact, many more than ninety-nine names—some so sacred to these faiths, the names can neither be written nor spoken.

Name trends come and go and often skip a generation or two. Names popular in the 1800s are seeing a resurgence today. A girl named Daisy would have been teased out of school in my generation, as it was considered only appropriate for dogs or ducks. Today, flower names are seeing a fashionable resurgence, particularly among celebrity and or new-age name movements.

Grandparents often feel they need a say in the naming of a grandchild. Beyond buying this book, a grandparent has absolutely no input. Sorry. That is the exclusive right of the parents. If the new mom and dad have reached an impasse between two names and simply can't decide, a grandparent may be asked their opinion, but they should know their choice will probably determine the name *not* chosen. Why? Because they are a generation past, and their grandchild, fresh from heaven, is the future.

For this volume, sacred names were culled from all over the world in research over the past two and a half years. It is by no means complete, or the only source of sacred names, but it is a good place to start with the basic name or name root, its most ancient origin, and the meaning most usually applied to it. These are names from every major and a few minor religions and belief systems. When you come across the term "Earth" listed as the source of a name, this just means it is a name related to the earth or mother nature; think new age. Some names include many versions or spellings of the same name. Others most commonly shortened I left for your taste and discretion. You may notice the name "Kai" was given every origin and meaning possible because I found it fascinating to have such universal acceptance. When the day comes to meet someone from another planet, don't be surprised if he introduces himself as Kai, a name probably understood on distant galaxies.

As men seem to take up the bulk of religious texts, the names of the women here include popular names from Yiddish to Zen Buddhist as well as the wives of prophets or shaman and more than a few ancient stories that may or may not be considered mythology. Island and Native American (shortened from here on as "Nat. Am.") names round out this broad field, but I must thank all the women who became Catholic Saints, without whom this volume would have been considerably shorter on the feminine side.

Reverently, quietly, when you are in a state of peace and love for all humankind, I hope you will prayerfully pick up this book and read through the names. Ponder them. Hum them to your unborn sons or daughters. Some will feel right. Most will not. List those you like in a notebook, then give this book to your companion to do the same when he or she is in a state of quiet contemplation. If you do this, you will receive the name of your child, even if it is not in this book—it will come to you. If you do this, your own blessed child will peer out from the veils of heaven and whisper the name on your heart.

We are, all of us, spiritual beings on an eternal journey of discovery. This is not our home but a short bump in the road. It is a place of trials and of testing. We are here to learn to love. What better way than by granting life to your children and helping them to safely chart the way back to our heavenly homes?

the names
feminine

name	source	meaning
Aarie	Hebrew	lion of God, angel
Aarona	Hebrew	strong
Aase	Norse	from a forest mountain
Aba	African	born on Thursday
Abha	Hindi	shine
Abia	Arabic	great one
Abida	Arabic	she who worships
Abigail	Hebrew	a father's joy
Abihail	Hebrew	Father is Lord
Abir	Arabic	a fragrant scent
Abishag	Hebrew	wise, knowing
Abishai	Hebrew	gift of God
Abishta	Hindi	woman of the home
Abital	Hebrew	morning dew
Acacia	Greek	flower
Acantha	Greek	sharp

A

Achall	Celtic	loving sister
Achsah	Egyptian	inspired
Ada	Hebrew	ornament
Adah	Hebrew	beautiful
Adara	Arabic	noble, virtuous
Ademia	Greek	alone
Adi	Hebrew	jewel
Adina	Norse	gentle, loving
Adinah	Hebrew	slender, delicate
Aditi	Hindi	mother of gods
Adona	Hebrew	Lord is God
Adonia	Greek	my Lord is God
Adora	Latin	beloved
Adoria	Latin	adored
Adria	Greek	dark-featured
Adriel	Hebrew	God's flock
Aesa	Norse	heavenly
Aesalina	Norse	heavenly woman
Agatha	Greek	good
Agathe	Norse	noble
Aglaia	Greek	splendor
Agnese	Greek	holy
Agneta	Norse	lamb
Agrata	Hindi	a leader
Ahinoam	Hebrew	pleasant
Ahlai	Hebrew	adornment
Aholah	Island	warm
Aholiamah	Hebrew	tabernacle
Aholibah	Hebrew	tabernacle
Ahuva	Hebrew	beloved
Aileen	Celtic	meadow
Ailen	Mapuche	little coal
Aimee	Latin	beloved
Ainakea	Island	white sand

Aine	Celtic	brilliant
Airlia	Greek	ethereal
Aisha	Arabic	alive
Ajala	Hindi	earth
Akuti	Hindi	princess
Alala	African	dreamer
Alba	Latin	dawn
Alberta	Latin	bright
Alcina	Greek	enchantment
Alderet	Arabic	angelic gift
Aleine	Celtic	alone
Alena	Greek	rock
Alessa	Greek	protector
Aleta	Greek	noble
Alethea	Greek	truth
Alexandra	Greek	protector of man
Alexia	Greek	protector of man
Alexica	Celtic	protect mankind
Alexis	Greek	protector of man
Alice	Celtic	noble
Alicia	Celtic	noble
Alida	Greek	adorned in beauty
Alix	Greek	defender of men
Aliza	Hebrew	joyful
Alka	Hindi	small girl
Alma	Latin	nourishing mother
Almond	Earth	hope
Alpa	Hindi	tiny little one
Alta	Latin	high grace
Althea	Greek	healer
Alyana	Greek	sun ray
Alysa	Greek	logical
Alysia	Greek	to bond
Alyssa	Greek	noble kind

Amaka	African	good
Amandine	Latin	lovable
Amara	Hindi	grass
Amarah	Greek	forever beautiful
Amber	Earth	warmth
Ambre	Arabic	a gem
Ambrosine	Latin	immortal
Amedea	Latin	beloved
Amel	Hebrew	aspire
Amelia	Latin	effort
Amelie	Latin	industrious
Amina	Arabic	faithful
Amira	Arabic	princess
Amit	Hebrew	friend
Amita	Hindi	limitless
Amoda	Hindi	happiness
Amoni	African	aspire
Amrita	Hindi	potion
Amy	Latin	loved
Anae	Arabic	crown
Anaelle	Hebrew	grace of God
Anais	Hebrew	graceful
Anandi	Hindi	happy
Anastasia	Greek	resurrection
Andrea	Egyptian	warrior
Andromeda	African	ruler of men
Anemone	Egyptian	wind
Angel	Greek	messenger
Angela	Latin	messenger
Angele	Celtic	high messenger
Angelina	Greek	messenger of God
Angell	Greek	messenger
Ania	Earth	orchid
Anissa	Greek	favored

Anna	Hebrew	grace
Annabelle	Hebrew	beautiful grace
Annalisa	Latin	God's bounty
Anndra	Egyptian	earth river's source
Anouk	Hebrew	favored grace
Answer	Earth	all-knowing
Anteia	Greek	ruler of the sea
Anthea	Greek	flowery
Aoife	Celtic	radiant one
Aphrodite	Greek	sea foam
Apolline	Greek	strength
Apphia	Hebrew	bountiful
April	Latin	to open
Arabella	Latin	answered prayer
Arcadia	Greek	small bear
Arella	Hebrew	messenger
Aretha	Greek	excellence
Aretina	Latin	righteous
Ariadne	Greek	most holy
Aricia	Greek	powerful
Ariel	Hebrew	lion of God
Ariela	Hebrew	lion of God
Ariella	Hebrew	lion of God
Artemis	Greek	moon girl
Artemisia	Arabic	full moon
Arya	Hindi	goddess
Asenath	Hebrew	father's daughter
Asherah	Hebrew	blessed, happy
Ashira	Hebrew	wealthy
Ashtoreth	Hebrew	star
Asia	Asian	east
Asha	Hindi	hope
Aspasia	Greek	welcome
Assia	Arabic	ascended

B

Astha	Hindi	hope
Astra	Greek	star
Astrid	Norse	God's fair beauty
Atara	Hebrew	diadem
Atarah	Hebrew	crown
Ateret	Hebrew	diadem
Athalia	Hebrew	God is praised
Athaliah	Hebrew	God is praised
Athena	Greek	wise
Ava	Hebrew	life
Avani	Hindi	earth
Aviv	Hebrew	spring
Aviva	Hebrew	springtime
Axelia	Greek	protector of all
Axelle	Latin	source of all life
Aya	Asian	colorful one
Ayala	Hebrew	gazelle
Ayelet	Hebrew	deer of dawn
AyoIa	Hebrew	deer
Azenor	Celtic	testimony
Azubah	Hebrew	forsaken

B

Barbara	Greek	foreign
Bala	Hindi	young girl
Basha	Hebrew	daughter of promise
Bashe	Hebrew	daughter of an oath
Basya	Hebrew	daughter of God
Batami	Hebrew	daughter of my nation

Bathsheba	Hebrew	daughter of an oath
Bathshua	Hebrew	daughter of opulence
Batia	Hebrew	daughter of God
Batsheva	Hebrew	daughter of an oath
Bayla	Hebrew	troubled
Beck	Norse	brook dweller
Bedelia	Celtic	strength, power
Bel	Sanskrit	sacred wood
Bela	Hindi	seashore
Bell	Hebrew	God's promise
Bella	Hebrew	my God is a vow
Bellanca	Greek	blonde
Belle	Hebrew	beautiful
Bernice	Greek	victory-bringer
Bess	Latin	God is my oath
Bethan	Celtic	God is my solemn vow
Bethany	Hebrew	house of figs
Bethel	Hebrew	house of the Lord
Bettina	Latin	my God is a vow
Beulah	Hebrew	bride
Beyla	Latin	by God
Beylke	Hebrew	white
Bhakti	Hindi	devotion
Bibiana	Latin	alive
Bilhah	Hebrew	shy, tender
Bina	Hebrew	insight
Bine	Hebrew	bee
Bithiah	Hebrew	daughter of God
Bliss	Earth	supreme happiness
Bluma	Hebrew	flower
Blume	Hebrew	flower
Bracha	Hebrew	blessing
Breeleigh	Celtic	meadow rose fairy
Breeze	Earth	carefree

Breindel	Hebrew	blessing
Briallan	Celtic	primrose
Bridget	Celtic	exalted one
Brina	Celtic	noble virtue
Brisen	Celtic	clarity
Bron	Celtic	fair
Bronte	Greek	thunder
Brooke	Latin	stream
Brynna	Celtic	rolling hill

Caitlin	Celtic	pure
Caitriona	Greek	clear
Calandra	Greek	lovely one
Calantha	Greek	lovely blossom
Callia	Greek	beautiful voice
Callidora	Greek	gift of beauty
Camelia	Latin	priests' helper
Camilla	Latin	ceremonial attendant
Camille	Latin	alter server
Candace	Latin	whiteness
Candice	Latin	clarity
Caoimhe	Celtic	gently beautiful
Capucine	Latin	cowl, covered
Cara	Latin	dear friend
Carla	Greek	free
Carmel	Hebrew	garden
Carmela	Latin	orchard
Caronwyn	Celtic	sweetheart
Cascadia	Greek	waterfall woman

Cassandra	Greek	entangler
Cassandre	Greek	prophetess
Cassia	Greek	like cinnamon
Casta	Hindi	good
Castalia	Greek	seawater
Catherine	Greek	pure
Catriona	Celtic	clear
Celandia	Greek	small bird
Celia	Latin	heaven
Chaima	Hebrew	joy, life
Charisma	Greek	divine gift
Charissa	Latin	grace
Charity	Latin	generous love
Charline	Latin	freedom
Charlotte	Latin	free
Charna	Hebrew	dark-featured
Chasya	Hebrew	protected by the Lord
Chava	Hebrew	life
Chaya	Hebrew	life
Cherise	Greek	cherry
Chesleigh	Celtic	meadow rose
Chiara	Latin	clear
Chloe	Greek	green
Christobel	Latin	follower of Christ
Ciara	Celtic	black
Circe	Greek	sun circle
Claire	Latin	bright
Clara	Latin	famous
Clarisant	Celtic	clear
Clarisse	Latin	bright
Claudia	Latin	visible miracle
Clea	Greek	glory
Clementine	Latin	merciful
Cleo	Greek	glory

Cliantha	Greek	flower of glory
Clo	Greek	young shoot
Colette	Greek	people of victory
Coline	Greek	young girl
Constance	Latin	steadfast
Cora	Greek	maiden
Coralie	Greek	maiden
Cosima	Greek	order, beauty
Cozbi	Hebrew	sliding away
Cressida	Greek	gold
Crisiant	Celtic	crystal
Crystyn	Greek	ice
Cushite	Arabic	coast
Cyleste	Latin	heavenly
Cynara	Greek	thistle
Cynthia	Greek	volcanic light
Cyrilla	Latin	ladylike

Daffodil	Greek	spring flower
Dafna	Hebrew	laurel
Daisy	Celtic	day's eye
Dalia	Norse	valley
Dalila	Hebrew	lovelorn
Damara	Greek	calf
Damaris	Hebrew	calf
Dana	Hebrew	judge
Daniella	Hebrew	God is my judge
Daphne	Greek	laurel
Dara	Hebrew	wise

Davan	Island	beloved
Daya	Sanskrit	compassion
Dayo	African	happiness
Deborah	Hebrew	bee
Deeba	Arabic	silk
Deena	Hebrew	leader
Deianira	Greek	destroyer
Delia	Celtic	fiery
Deliah	Hebrew	delicate
Delilah	Hebrew	lovelorn
Delphine	Greek	dolphin
Demetria	Greek	whole grains
Dena	Hebrew	valley
Denise	Latin	flower
Desdemona	Greek	tragic
Despina	Greek	lady
Destiny	Latin	certain fortune
Deva	Sanskrit	gift
Devorah	Sanskrit	victory
Dew	Earth	morning mist
Dianthe	Latin	divine
Diarria	Greek	healthy
Diblaim	Hebrew	fig cakes
Diena	Hebrew	justified ruler
Dinah	Hebrew	judged
Dionne	Greek	follower
Divinity	Sanskrit	flawless
Divorah	Hebrew	honeybee
Divya	Hindi	heavenly
Donata	Latin	given
Dora	Greek	all gifts
Dorcas	Greek	female deer
Doria	Greek	gift
Dorinda	Greek	gift

Doris	Greek	gift
Dorothy	Greek	gift of God
Dove	Earth	peace bird
Dream	Earth	deep-thinker
Drew	Celtic	wise
Drucilla	Latin	watered by dew
Drusilla	Greek	strong, sturdy
Dvoire	Sanskrit	black
Dwyn	Celtic	pleasant
Dyna	Greek	athlete

Eartha	Earth	mother earth
Ebony	Egyptian	deep-black wood
Edda	Norse	poetry
Eden	Hebrew	delight
Edha	Sanskrit	sacred
Edna	Hebrew	renewer, seed
Edria	Island	mighty
Effie	Greek	singer
Efrat	Hebrew	honored
Eglah	Hebrew	heifer
Egyptus	Greek	fortress, daughter of Ptaú
Eidel	Hebrew	gentle
Eileen	Celtic	light, glowing
Eirene	Greek	peace
Ela	Island	black, shining
Elana	Hebrew	spirited
Elea	Greek	shining light
Eleanor	Greek	God is light

Elenola	Island	bright
Electra	Greek	radiant light
Elektra	Greek	bright and shining one
Elena	Greek	sunray
Eleni	Greek	sunray
Eletta	Celtic	elfin, small
Elga	Celtic	holy
Eliana	Hebrew	God's answer
Elicia	Greek	truthful
Elina	Greek	shining light
Eline	Celtic	sunlight
Eliora	Hebrew	God is my light
Elisa	Hebrew	God's promise
Elisabeth	Hebrew	God is my oath
Elise	Hebrew	God's promise
Elisha	Hebrew	God is my salvation
Elisheba	Hebrew	God is my oath
Elisheva	Hebrew	God is my oath
Elissa	Greek	from the blessed isles
Elita	Latin	chosen one
Eliza	Hebrew	God's promise
Elizabeth	Hebrew	my God is a vow
Elke	Celtic	noble
Elkie	Norse	lookout, mainsail girl
Ella	Greek	torch, bright light
Ellie	Greek	exalted
Ellimae	Norse	old soul
Elma	Norse	protection
Elmira	Arabic	noble princess
Elodie	Greek	marsh flower
Eloise	Norse	warrior
Elonore	Greek	compassionate
Elsa	Hebrew	God's promise
Elspeth	Hebrew	devoted to God

Elvina	Celtic	little, elfin
Ema	Celtic	universal
Emanuela	Hebrew	God is with us
Eme	Island	loved
Emeline	Norse	industrious
Emilia	Latin	to emulate
Emilie	Hebrew	effort
Emily	Latin	eager
Emma	Latin	complete
Emmy	Latin	to emulate
Emy	Latin	hard worker
Ena	Celtic	fiery
Endora	Hebrew	fountain
Enid	Celtic	fair, lovely
Ennis	Celtic	meadow island
Enola	Nat. Am.	solitary
Enora	Greek	honor
Eos	Greek	dawn
Ephah	Hebrew	to fly
Ephratah	Hebrew	fruitful
Ephrath	Hebrew	fruitful
Erena	Greek	torch
Erin	Celtic	emerald island
Ertha	Celtic	earth
Esme	Latin	love
Esmee	Celtic	emerald stone
Estelle	Latin	star
Ester	Latin	star
Esther	Hebrew	star
Ethel	Celtic	righteous
Ethereal	Earth	other-worldly
Eudocia	Greek	good gift
Eudora	Greek	good present
Eugenia	Greek	of noble descent

Eulalia	Greek	articulate
Eunice	Latin	victory
Euodia	Greek	fragrant
Euphemia	Greek	well-spoken
Eurielle	Celtic	angelic
Eurwen	Celtic	fair as gold
Eva	Hebrew	life
Evadine	Greek	thriving valley
Evadne	Greek	healthy
Evangelia	Greek	bearer of good news
Evangelina	Greek	good news
Evangeline	Greek	good news
Eve	Hebrew	life
Evelyn	Celtic	light, fire
Ever	Earth	always, forever
Evie	Hebrew	living, life
Ewa	Hebrew	mother
Ewe	Hebrew	lamb God hears

Faiga	Hebrew	bird
Faigel	Hebrew	bird
Faith	Latin	confidence
Farah	Arabic	cheerful
Faustina	Latin	good fortune
Faustine	Latin	fortunate
Fawn	Latin	young deer
Fedora	Greek	gift of God
Feiga	Hebrew	bird
Fiona	Celtic	fair, beautiful

Fionn	Celtic	fair and white
Fira	Celtic	little fire
Firinne	Celtic	pure truth
Flavia	Latin	golden hair
Flavie	Latin	golden
Flo	Latin	in bloom
Flora	Latin	flower
Florence	Latin	charming
Flower	Earth	a bloom
Fon	Celtic	to tease
Frayda	Hebrew	joy
Freya	Norse	noble woman
Frienda	Celtic	little, beloved
Fruma	Hebrew	deeply pious

Gabriela	Latin	God is my might
Gabriella	Latin	strength of God
Gabrielle	Hebrew	heroine of God
Gada	Hebrew	fortunate
Gaea	Greek	of the earth
Gaho	Nat. Am.	motherly
Gail	Hebrew	father's joy
Gala	Norse	merrymaker
Galatea	Greek	fair complected
Galena	Greek	peaceful
Gali	Hebrew	fountain
Galia	Latin	calm
Gamada	African	pleasing
Gamila	Arabic	elegant woman

Gana	Hebrew	garden woman
Ganga	Hindi	river
Garbina	Latin	pure
Gavina	Latin	white falcon
Gayla	Celtic	rejoicing
Gayna	Celtic	soft, white
Geba	Hebrew	hill dweller
Gefen	Hebrew	vine
Gefjun	Norse	prophetess
Geila	Hebrew	bringer of joy
Gelasia	Greek	laughing girl
Gemma	Latin	precious
Gen	Asian	spring
Genesis	Hebrew	beginning
Genet	African	paradise garden
Genista	Latin	lovely plant
Gentle	Earth	delicate, soft
Georgette	Greek	worker of earth
Georgia	Greek	farmer
Gerd	Norse	protected
Germaine	Latin	sisterly
Geva	Hebrew	farmer
Gevira	Hebrew	highborn
Ghada	Arabic	beautiful girl
Gianna	Latin	god is gracious
Gila	Hebrew	forever joyous
Gifty	African	God's gift
Gildas	Celtic	Lord's servant
Gilead	Hebrew	mountain testimony
Giorsal	Celtic	assistant
Giovanna	Latin	God is gracious
Gisella	Latin	God's promise
Gita	Hindi	beautiful song
Gitel	Hebrew	good

Glenda	Celtic	good, fair
Glenys	Celtic	holy woman
Gna	Norse	handmaid
Goldea	Celtic	precious
Gomer	Hebrew	to finish
Grace	Latin	God's favor
Gracie	Latin	God's thanks
Gratia	Latin	God's blessing
Gunoda	Celtic	blessed
Gwen	Celtic	fair, holy
Gwyn	Celtic	white, blessed
Gwyneth	Celtic	happiness
Gytha	Celtic	treasured
Gzifa	African	at peace

Habbai	Arabic	much loved
Hadar	Hebrew	splendor, glory
Hadas	Hebrew	myrtle flower
Hadassah	Hebrew	myrtle tree
Hadria	Latin	walled city
Hady	Greek	soulful
Hadya	Arabic	spiritual guide
Hafwen	Celtic	summer
Hagar	Hebrew	traveler
Hagen	Celtic	youthful
Haggith	Hebrew	dancer
Haiba	African	charming
Haidee	Greek	modest
Hailee	Old English	straw meadow

Haimi	Island	truth-seeker
Haiwee	Nat. Am.	dove of peace
Hala	Arabic	moon halo, sweet
Hale	Arabic	halo
Haletta	Greek	meadow girl
Haley	Latin	breathe out
Halia	Island	remembrance
Haliaka	Island	leader
Halina	Greek	calm, light
Halle	Norse	rock, home ruler
Halli	Greek	hallowed
Hallie	Greek	home ruler
Hamutal	Hebrew	morning dew
Hanae	Asian	flower blessing
Hannah	Hebrew	favored of God
Happi	African	happiness, fortune
Harmony	Latin	concord, harmony
Harriet	Latin	hearth-keeper
Haya	Hebrew	alive, living
Haylee	Latin	breathe out
Hayley	Norse	hero
Hazel	Hebrew	God sees
Heaven	Hebrew	height, elevation
Heidi	Norse	bright, clear
Heidrun	Norse	provider
Helah	Hebrew	rust
Helam	Hebrew	prosperous
Helen	Greek	shining light
Helena	Greek	sun ray
Heli	Greek	light
Hella	Norse	blessed, holy
Helle	Greek	bright and shining one
Helsa	Norse	bountiful
Henda	Hebrew	gracious

Hende	Greek	fair, yellow
Hephzibah	Hebrew	delight
Hera	Greek	chosen, blessed
Herodias	Greek	watch, monitor
Hila	Greek	love
Hilja	Norse	silent one
Hinto	Nat. Am.	blue eyes
Hiriwa	Island	silver girl
Hodesh	Hebrew	new moon birth
Hoglah	Hebrew	festival dance
Holi	Hindi	spring colors
Hollie	Celtic	to prick
Holly	Earth	holly berry
Honey	Earth	sweet health
Honna	Latin	honorable
Hope	Hebrew	high expectations
Hosanna	Hebrew	high praise
Hoshi	Asian	shining star
Hova	African	centered
Howell	Celtic	to shine
Hubab	Arabic	focused
Huda	Arabic	good guidance
Hudel	Norse	lovable
Hudes	Hebrew	of Judea
Hudi	Arabic	chooses right
Huhana	Island	graceful lily
Huldah	Hebrew	weasel
Humita	Nat. Am.	corn-sheller
Hurit	Nat. Am.	a beauty
Huyana	Nat. Am.	rain daughter
Hyacinth	Greek	fragrant flower
Hyades	Greek	ocean daughter
Hyderia	Greek	water woman
Hye	Asian	graceful woman

Hypatia	Greek	supreme intellect
Hye	Asian	intelligent, wise
Hyeon	Asian	virtuous
Hywel	Celtic	supreme eminence

Iamar	Arabic	of the moon
Ianthe	Greek	violet flower
Ianna	Celtic	gracious
Ida	Greek	diligent
Idaa	Hindi	earth woman
Idalika	Arabic	royal woman
Idelle	Celtic	bountiful
Idil	Latin	pleasant woman
Idona	Norse	fresh-faced girl
Idony	Norse	reborn
Ife	African	loved, loves
Ignatia	Latin	burning brightly
Ihab	Arabic	gift of God
Iku	Asian	nurturer
Ilana	Hebrew	from the trees
Ilesha	Hindi	of the earth
Iliana	Greek	shining light
Ilima	Hebrew	flower
Ilona	Greek	bright torch
Ilori	African	treasured child
Ilyse	Greek	noble born
Imane	Arabic	faith, belief
Imma	Arabic	water-pourer
Imogen	Celtic	maiden

Ina	Island	moon goddess
Inaki	Asian	generous nature
Inara	Arabic	shining light
Inari	Asian	a success
Inarie	Norse	lady of the lake
Inas	Arabic	sociable, friendly
Inaya	Arabic	guardian
Ines	Greek	pure, holy
Indre	Hindi	splendor
Infinity	Hindi	immeasurable
Inis	Celtic	island dweller
Inoa	Greek	island
Iona	Norse	island
Iorwen	Celtic	lovely girl
Irene	Greek	peace
Iridessa	Arabic	glowing, radiant
Iris	Celtic	rainbow
Irit	Hebrew	flowering plant
Isabella	Latin	consecrated
Isabis	African	beautiful child
Isadora	Greek	gift of Isis
Isairis	Latin	lively
Isamu	Asian	energetic
Isaura	Greek	soft breeze
Iscah	Hebrew	observant
Ishtar	Hebrew	star
Isi	Nat. Am.	young deer
Isis	Egyptian	goddess
Isla	Celtic	island
Ismat	Arabic	safeguard
Ismene	Greek	treasured
Isobel	Hebrew	God's promise
Isra	Arabic	evening traveller
Ito	Asian	delicate girl

Iudita	Island	affectionate
Iulia	Latin	sky daughter
Ixchel	Mayan	rainbow woman
Izolde	Greek	philosophical
Izso	Hebrew	saved by God
Izusa	Nat. Am.	white stone

Jace	Greek	healer
Jacinda	Latin	hyacinth
Jacinta	Greek	hyacinth
Jade	Hebrew	well known
Jael	Hebrew	mountain goat
Jaffa	Hebrew	beautiful
Jaha	African	dignified
Jaira	Hebrew	she shines
Jala	Arabic	clarity
Jalila	Arabic	exalted
Jamie	Hebrew	supplanter
Janae	Hebrew	answered prayer
Janan	Arabic	heart and soul
Jane	Hebrew	God is gracious
Jannat	Arabic	garden of heaven
Jarah	Hebrew	kind, sweet
Jarina	Greek	farmer
Jasmine	Arabic	fragrant
Javana	Hebrew	Greek woman
Jaya	Hindi	victorious woman
Jaydra	Arabic	filled with goodness
Jayla	Arabic	charitable

Jean	Hebrew	God is gracious
Jecoliah	Hebrew	God provides
Jedida	Hebrew	greatly loved
Jehan	Arabic	beautiful flower
Jehoaddan	Hebrew	Lord's delight
Jehosheba	Hebrew	God's oath
Jemima	Hebrew	dove
Jemina	Hebrew	understood
Jena	Arabic	small bird
Jendayi	Egyptian	thankful one
Jenis	Hebrew	beginning
Jeriel	Hebrew	God sees
Jerioth	Hebrew	tent, curtains
Jerusha	Hebrew	faithful wife
Jessica	Hebrew	He sees all
Jethra	Hebrew	abundance
Jewel	Latin	precious
Jezreel	Hebrew	Lord provides
Jie	Asian	chaste
Jin	Asian	golden child
Jina	African	named one
Jiva	Hindi	immortal essence
Joanna	Hebrew	God is gracious
Jobey	Hebrew	persecuted
Jocelyn	Latin	cheerful
Jochebed	Hebrew	God is her glory
Joda	Hebrew	ancestor of Christ
Joelle	Hebrew	God is willing
Jokim	Hebrew	blessed by God
Jolan	Greek	violet flower
Jora	Hebrew	autumn rose
Jord	Norse	earth goddess
Jordana	Hebrew	reversed river
Jorunn	Norse	loves horses

Josephine	Hebrew	God will add
Jovita	Latin	sky daughter
Joy	Latin	a delight
Juanita	Latin	God is gracious
Juba	African	Monday's child
Jubilee	Hebrew	rejoicing
Juci	Hebrew	praised
Juda	Arabic	goodness
Judith	Hebrew	woman of Judea
Juji	African	greatly loved
Julia	Latin	sky daughter
Juliette	Latin	youthful
June	Latin	born in June
Junia	Latin	youthful
Juniper	Latin	fragrant shrub
Juno	Latin	marriage goddess
Justine	Latin	upright

K

Kabye	African	petite woman
Kachina	Nat. Am.	spiritual dancer
Kadin	Arabic	beloved companion
Kadisha	Hebrew	holy woman
Kaede	Asian	maple leaf
Kafi	African	well behaved
Kai	Island	sea woman
Kaia	Asian	restful yew tree
Kaila	Hebrew	laurel crown
Kailani	Island	of sky and sea
Kaimana	Island	diamond

Kaimi	Island	seeker
Kalama	Island	light
Kalani	Island	from the heavens
Kalanit	Hebrew	flower
Kalea	Island	flower wreath
Kalei	Island	flower wreath
Kali	Hindi	black
Kalika	Greek	rosebud
Kalilah	Arabic	darling girl
Kalla	Celtic	flowing water
Kalliope	Greek	beautiful voice
Kalonice	Greek	victorious beauty
Kama	Hindi	loves, loved
Kamalei	Island	beloved child
Kamaria	African	of the moon
Kamea	Island	sweet darling
Kameli	Island	honeybee
Kamil	Arabic	perfect one
Kani	Asian	powerful woman
Kanani	Island	beautiful one
Kanda	Nat. Am.	magical woman
Kani	Island	sound
Kaniz	Arabic	servant girl
Kanoa	Island	free one
Kanti	Nat. Am.	sings well
Kanti	Sanskrit	lovely one
Kapila	Sanskrit	reddish brown
Kapua	Island	flower blossom
Kara	Greek	pure
Karen	Greek	pure
Karena	Greek	pure
Karima	Arabic	noble
Karissa	Greek	grace, kindness
Karmel	Latin	fruitful orchard

Karmen	Latin	beautiful song
Karmiti	Nat. Am.	from the trees
Karsten	Greek	anointed one
Kasen	Norse	pure, chaste
Kasi	Hindi	shining city
Kasinda	African	girl with twin sisters
Kassia	Greek	pure
Kate	Greek	pure
Katherine	Greek	pure
Katriel	Hebrew	crowned by God
Kauket	Egyptian	ancient goddess
Kawena	Island	glowing
Kay	Greek	pure, virtuous
Kayin	African	long-awaited girl
Kayle	Arabic	crowned with laurel
Kazia	Island	cinnamon-like
Keala	Island	path, road
Keavy	Celtic	grace, beauty
Kefira	Hebrew	lioness
Keiki	Island	descendant
Keilana	Island	adored one
Keilani	Island	heaven, sky
Keira	Celtic	black onyx
Kekona	Island	graceful
Kelly	Celtic	bright-headed
Kenza	Celtic	fair one
Keona	Celtic	from the sea's edge
Ketaki	Hindi	golden daughter
Keturah	Hebrew	fragrance
Kezia	Hebrew	cassia tree
Kiele	Celtic	fragrant flower
Kilia	Island	heaven
Kinneret	Hebrew	harp
Kirati	Hindi	mountaintop

Kiri	Hindi	amaranth flower
Kirima	Eskimo	from the hill
Kirsten	Norse	follower of Christ
Kishi	African	from the hills
Kismet	Arabic	lot or portion
Kissa	African	joyful
Kissa	Norse	pure joy
Kolina	Norse	maiden
Komala	Hindi	tender, delicate
Kreindel	Hebrew	crown
Kristabelle	Latin	gem, ice
Krysia	Norse	follower of Christ
Kunani	Island	beautiful one
Kynthia	Greek	from the mountain

Lacey	Latin	lacelike
Laka	Island	dancers
Lakia	Arabic	treasured
Lalia	Greek	well spoken
Laly	Greek	soft talk
Lamis	Arabic	soft skin
Lana	Greek	bright torch
Landra	Latin	wise counsel
Lang	Norse	tall woman
Lani	Island	heavenly
Lanka	Hindi	from island fortress
Lanza	Latin	noble and willing
Lapidoth	Hebrew	enlightened
Lapis	Egyptian	blue gemstone

Lara	Latin	cheerful woman
Larenta	Latin	earth goddess
Laria	Greek	star goddess
Larissa	Latin	cheerful, lighthearted
Laulani	Island	heavenly
Laura	Latin	protection
Lauren	Latin	the bay
Laurine	Latin	laurel plant
Lavinia	Latin	motherly
Layla	Arabic	beauty of nightfall
Layna	Greek	truth
Le	Asian	bringer of joy
Leah	Hebrew	hard worker
Leana	Greek	delicate sunlight
Leandra	Greek	lioness
Leane	Celtic	shining light
Leeba	Hebrew	dearly loved
Leela	Hindi	accomplished actor
Lehava	Hebrew	little flame
Leiko	Island	small flower
Leila	Arabic	dark-haired beauty
Leilani	Island	child of heaven
Leitha	Greek	forgetful
Lemuela	Hebrew	devoted to God
Lena	Greek	shining light
Lenis	Latin	silky skin
Leona	Latin	lioness
Leonora	Greek	shining light
Leotee	Nat. Am.	wildflower
Lequoia	Nat. Am.	giant redwood
Leta	Latin	joyful
Letha	Latin	bringer of joy
Levana	Latin	protector of infants
Levia	Hebrew	alliance-maker

Levina	Latin	lightning bolt
Lewa	African	beautiful woman
Lexie	Greek	mankind's defender
Li	Asian	strength, sharpness
Liat	Celtic	northern light
Liba	Hebrew	weak, old
Libby	Hebrew	bountiful God
Libe	Latin	olive tree
Life	Earth	robust, healthy
Light	Earth	bright, shining
Lila	Arabic	night lily
Lilah	Arabic	lovelorn
Lilia	Latin	lilies
Lillian	Latin	flower
Lilou	Latin	lilies
Lily	Earth	lily flower
Lily-Rose	Earth	flowers
Lina	Arabic	delicate, compassionate
Lina	Norse	sacred woman
Lindsay	Celtic	dark lake, mysterious
Ling	Asian	sound of dawning
Linnea	Norse	lime flower
Lior	Hebrew	light I see
Liora	Hebrew	God's gift, light
Liraz	Hebrew	my secret
Lirit	Hebrew	musically talented
Liron	Hebrew	song is my joy
Lisa	Hebrew	bountiful God
Lise	Hebrew	my God is my vow
Lisi	Latin	a noble kind
Lishan	African	awarded
Lison	Greek	perfection
Liv	Norse	protector
Livana	Hebrew	white moon

Livna	Hebrew	white, bright
Livnat	Hebrew	bright moon
Livonah	Hebrew	vibrant, full of life
Liya	Hebrew	Lord's daughter
Liza	Hebrew	bountiful God
Lizandra	Hebrew	white moon
Loane	Arabic	friendly
Lofn	Norse	goddess
Logan	Celtic	from the hollow
Lois	Greek	superior woman
Lokalia	Island	rose garland
Loki	Norse	a trickster
Lola	Latin	sorrows
Lomasi	Nat. Am.	beautiful flower
Lora	Latin	laurel crown
Lotus	Greek	water lily
Lou	Latin	bright
Louane	Arabic	friendly
LouAnn	Greek	flower blossom
Louanne	Hebrew	God is gracious
Louisa	Latin	fame
Louise	Latin	loud
Louna	Latin	moon
Lourdes	French	a miracle
Lovella	Nat. Am.	a soft spirit
Luana	Island	content
Luba	Hebrew	dearly loved
Lucerne	Latin	all is light
Lucie	Latin	light
Lucile	Latin	light of God
Lucretia	Latin	light-bringer
Lucy	Latin	light
Lulani	Island	heaven-sent
Lulu	African	precious pearl

Luna	Latin	moon
Lundy	Celtic	marshland
Lur	Latin	of the earth
Lux	Latin	lady of light
Luyu	Nat. Am.	dovelike
Luz	Arabic	moonlight
Lya	Asian	chilly
Lydia	Greek	beautiful woman
Lymekia	Greek	wolf
Lylou	African	valuable pearl
Lyna	Greek	filtered light
Lyra	Greek	musical lyre
Lyron	Greek	song, singing
Lysandra	Greek	helper of mankind
Lyssan	Greek	defender of all

Maachah	Hebrew	oppressed
Maarath	Hebrew	desolate land
Maasiai	Hebrew	God's worker
Maat	Egyptian	truth, order, justice
Maath	Hebrew	small woman
Maayan	Hebrew	spring
Mabina	Celtic	nimble
Macaria	Latin	blessed one
Macha	Nat. Am.	light or aurora
Machi	Asian	a friend
Machiko	Asian	truth-taught child
Mackenna	Celtic	daughter of beauty
Mada	Arabic	pathfinder

Madana	African	the healer
Madeline	Hebrew	woman of Magdala
Madini	African	precious gem
Madonna	Latin	my lady, virgin
Maeko	Asian	honest child
Maelie	Asian	industrious
Maeline	Hebrew	woman of Magdala
Maely	Hebrew	sweet honey
Maeva	Celtic	tall, fair
Maeve	Celtic	tall, fair
Magdalena	Greek	of Magdala
Mahala	Nat. Am.	tender woman
Mahalath	Arabic	marrow
Mahina	Hebrew	tender one
Mahari	African	forgiveness
Mahola	Hebrew	love of dance
Mahsa	Arabic	moonlight
Maia	Latin	great one
Maibe	Egyptian	dignified woman
Maiki	Asian	flower dancer
Maille	Celtic	star of the sea
Mairwen	Celtic	fair, delicate
Mailys	Greek	honeybee
Maisie	Celtic	child of light
Maissa	Arabic	graceful
Maisy	Greek	pearl
Maka	Nat. Am.	wild goose
Makala	Island	myrtle flower
Makani	Island	of the wind
Makara	Island	Pleiadian star
Makea	Norse	sweet one
Malana	Island	buoyant light
Malinda	Latin	sweet
Malka	Hebrew	queenly

Malle	Celtic	river plant flower
Malu	Island	peaceful
Maluna	Island	to rise above
Maluhia	Island	restful safety
Malulani	Island	under peaceful skies
Malys	Asian	blossom
Malva	Greek	soft and slender
Malvinia	Latin	beloved friend
Mamo	Island	yellow flower
Mamiko	Asian	sea daughter
Mana	Island	charismatic woman
Manal	Arabic	accomplished woman
Manar	Arabic	woman of light
Manasa	Hindi	mental powers
Manel	Hebrew	God with us
Manika	Sanskrit	mind is a jewel
Manolita	Latin	God with us
Manon	Hebrew	beloved
Mansi	Nat. Am.	a picked flower
Manto	Greek	prophetess
Mara	Hebrew	sorrowful
Maram	Arabic	wished for
Marcella	Latin	planet Mars
Marenda	Latin	admirable woman
Margaret	Greek	a pearl
Margot	Latin	child of light
Mari	Hebrew	wished-for daughter
Mariah	Latin	star of the sea
Mariama	African	gift of God
Marie	Latin	star of the sea
Marifa	Arabic	great knowledge
Marigold	Earth	golden flower
Marina	Latin	woman of the sea
Marion	Hebrew	bitter

Marsha	Latin	planet Mars
Martha	Aramaic	house mistress
Marwa	Arabic	fragrant plant
Mary	Latin	star of the sea
Maryam	Greek	uncertain
Masami	African	commanding woman
Masika	Egyptian	rainstorm-born
Massarra	Arabic	full of happiness
Matana	Hebrew	gift of God
Matilda	Norse	battle maiden
Maurissa	Latin	dark beauty
Mave	Celtic	bringer of joy
Mavelle	Celtic	songbird
May	Latin	May-born
Maya	Hindi	an illusion
Mayim	Hebrew	unique
Maytal	Hebrew	dew drops
Mazel	Hebrew	blessed or lucky
Meara	Celtic	filled with happiness
Meda	Nat. Am.	prophetess
Medeba	Hebrew	from quiet waters
Medora	Greek	a wise ruler
Meena	Hindi	a small fish
Megan	Greek	a pearl
Megara	Greek	wife of strength
Mehetabel	Hebrew	joyous
Mei	Latin	great one
Melaina	Greek	dark beauty
Melanctha	Greek	black flower
Melanie	Greek	dark beauty
Mele	Island	beloved
Melek	Arabic	heavenly messenger
Melia	Celtic	worker
Melina	Greek	honeybee

41

Melinda	Latin	worker bee
Melissa	Greek	honeybee
Melita	Greek	honeybee
Melka	Greek	dark beauty
Melody	Greek	beautiful song
Melva	Celtic	chief
Mem	Greek	established
Menaka	Hindi	heavenly maiden
Mene	Hebrew	deeds were weighed
Menefer	Egyptian	dwells in beauty
Merab	Hebrew	abundant
Mercey	Celtic	compassionate
Merry	Celtic	lighthearted, joyful
Mesi	Egyptian	woman of the waters
Metea	Greek	a gentle woman
Metin	Greek	wise, a counselor
Metis	Greek	industrious
Mia	Latin	star of the sea
Miakoda	Nat. Am.	power of the moon
Micah	Hebrew	humble
Michaela	Celtic	close to God
Michal	Hebrew	humble
Michelina	Celtic	close to God
Michewa	Tibetan	sent from heaven
Migdalia	Hebrew	from the high tower
Miki	Island	nimble
Mila	Celtic	clever, industrious
Milan	Latin	gracious, helpful
Milcah	Hebrew	queen
Miliani	Island	gentle caress
Millicent	Latin	highborn strength
Millo	Latin	gracious power
Mina	Celtic	greatly loved
Minda	Hindi	great knowledge

Minerva	Latin	wisdom
Ming	Asian	brightness, light
Minya	Nat. Am.	older sister
Mio	Asian	great strength
Mirabel	Latin	rare beauty, wonderful
Miracle	Earth	established truth
Mirena	Latin	of the sea
Miriam	Hebrew	star of the sea
Misty	Earth	morning dew
Mitena	Nat. Am.	new moon birth
Moana	Island	ocean woman
Mocha	Arabic	sweet as chocolate
Modesty	Latin	without conceit
Moema	Nat. Am.	sweet
Mohala	Island	unfolding flower
Molly	Celtic	perfect one
Monca	Celtic	great wisdom
Monica	Latin	advisor
Monisha	Hindi	intelligence
Moon	Asian	letters, writing
Mor	Celtic	exceptional woman
Morgane	Celtic	sea circle, round
Moriah	Hebrew	taught of God
Mor	Celtic	exceptional woman
Moraika	Incan	heavenly messenger
Moreh	Hebrew	great archer, teacher
Moriah	Hebrew	God is my teacher
Mosi	Egyptian	firstborn
Moya	Arabic	great
Muirne	Celtic	beloved
Mulan	Asian	magnolia blossom
Muna	Arabic	God with me
Muriel	Arabic	myrrh plant
Muta	Latin	silent one

Mya	Hindi	an illusion
Myisha	Arabic	lively, colorful
Myka	Hebrew	humble one
Myla	Celtic	merciful, kind
Myrna	Celtic	loved one
Mwynen	Celtic	gentle one
Mylene	Celtic	merciful
Myra	Greek	fragrant oil
Myriam	Hebrew	star of the sea
Myrtle	Latin	sacred evergreen

Naama	Hebrew	attractive woman
Naarah	Hebrew	young girl
Nadie	Arabic	delicate
Nadda	Arabic	generous
Nadifa	African	between seasons
Nadira	Arabic	rare
Nagge	Hebrew	radiant
Nagina	Arabic	precious pearl
Naible	Celtic	lovely little one
Naida	Arabic	delicate, tender
Naki	African	firstborn daughter
Nala	Latin	olive tree
Nalani	Island	calm skies
Nana	Island	spring star
Nandita	Hindi	delightful daughter
Nani	Greek	charming woman
Naomi	Hebrew	pleasant
Narcissa	Greek	daffodil

Narda	Latin	anointed in fragrance
Narella	Greek	intelligent, bright
Naria	Asian	thunderbolt
Nascha	Nat. Am.	owllike
Nasha	African	soft rain
Nata	Latin	strong swimmer
Natalie	Latin	Christmas
Nava	Hebrew	lovely
Naveen	Celtic	pleasant
Navlin	Hindi	loving, youth
Navya	Hindi	youthful
Nayan	Hindi	beautiful eyes
Nayeli	Nat. Am.	I love you
Nea	Celtic	mountain flower
Neala	Celtic	champion
Nebula	Latin	woman of mists
Nehushta	Hebrew	copper-colored
Nellie	Greek	light, sunray
Nechama	Hebrew	comforter
Neci	Latin	impetuous
Nediva	Hebrew	noble, giving
Neena	Hindi	beautiful eyes
Nehara	Hebrew	born of the light
Neith	Egyptian	hunter, seeker
Nemetona	Celtic	sacred grove
Neo	African	gift of God
Neola	Greek	youthful
Neoma	Greek	new moon
Nera	Hebrew	flickering candle
Neria	Greek	sea daughter
Nerita	Greek	woman of the sea
Nessa	Hebrew	miracle child
Neta	Nat. Am.	worthy of trust
Neva	Latin	snow-covered

Nia	African	brightness, purpose
Niamh	Celtic	bright woman
Nicia	Latin	victorious
Nicole	Greek	victorious people
Nida	Nat. Am.	elfin, delicate
Nikita	Greek	unconquered
Nike	Greek	victory
Nina	Nat. Am.	spicy, fiery
Ning	Asian	peaceful
Ninon	Hebrew	grace
Nini	African	solid, strong
Nipa	Hindi	gentle brook
Nira	Hebrew	sower, plowed field
Nirit	Hebrew	flowering plant
Nisa	Arabic	honest woman
Nisha	Hindi	born at night
Nishan	African	award-winner
Nissa	Hebrew	educator
Nisse	Norse	friendly, elfin
Nita	Hebrew	grace
Nitika	Nat. Am.	precious gem
Nitya	Hindi	eternal beauty
Nitzan	Hebrew	sprout
Noa	Hebrew	active woman
Noadiah	Hebrew	God's construction
Nola	Celtic	white shoulder
Noelani	Island	mist of heaven
Noelia	Latin	day of birth
Nogah	Hebrew	bright, lustrous
Noma	African	homegrown
Noni	Celtic	northern lights, aurora
Nora	Greek	shining light, integrity
Norna	Norse	destiny, direction
Nour	Arabic	light, truth

Nubia	Egyptian	gentle cloud
Nura	Arabic	woman of light
Nurit	Hebrew	red and yellow blossoms
Nyah	African	tenacious, determined
Nyx	Greek	night goddess

Oamra	Arabic	moon daughter
Oanez	Greek	pure, chaste
Oba	African	river goddess
Obelia	Greek	pillar of strength
Oberon	Latin	divine
Oceana	Greek	river maiden
Ode	Egyptian	traveler
Odela	Greek	sweet melody
Odessa	Greek	wanderer
Odina	Latin	highest mountain
Ogin	Nat. Am.	wild rose
Ohela	Hebrew	tent dweller
Oheo	Nat. Am.	beautiful woman
Ofira	Arabic	sandalwood
Ofra	Hebrew	fawn
Oira	Latin	one who prays
Okalani	Island	from the heavens
Ola	Norse	descendant
Olathe	Nat. Am.	lovely young girl
Olina	Norse	northern lights
Olisa	Nat. Am.	devoted to God
Olivia	Latin	peaceful one
Olwen	Celtic	path-lighter

O

Olympia	Greek	from Mt. Olympus
Omega	Greek	final great one
Ona	Hebrew	filled with grace
Oni	Nat. Am.	on sacred ground
Oona	Celtic	pure, chaste
Opa	Nat. Am.	wise owl
Opal	Sanskrit	treasured jewel
Ophel	Hebrew	from temple hill
Ophelia	Greek	helpful, empathetic
Ophira	Hebrew	golden
Ophrah	Hebrew	a fawn
Ora	Latin	prayerful
Orin	Celtic	dark beauty
Orla	Celtic	golden one
Orphne	Greek	swimming girl
Orthia	Greek	straight path
Orzona	Hebrew	strength of God
Oseye	Egyptian	filled with happiness
Otrera	Greek	tall, strong woman
Ovida	Hebrew	worshipper of God
Oya	Nat. Am.	called of God
Ozera	Hebrew	meritorious woman

Padma	Hindi	lotus flower
Paka	African	catlike woman
Pala	Nat. Am.	sea-maiden
Palesa	African	flower, delicate
Pallas	Greek	wisdom, understanding
Palmira	Latin	white palms, dove

Paloma	Latin	dovelike
Pamela	Greek	all honey, sweet
Pandara	Hindi	a good wife
Pandora	Greek	talented, gifted
Panthea	Greek	of the gods and goddesses
Panya	Latin	a small child
Para	Norse	household spirits
Parvani	Hindi	full moon
Pavarti	Hindi	mountain daughter
Paschel	African	spiritual woman
Pasha	Greek	woman of the sea
Pati	African	one who fishes
Patia	Latin	open-minded woman
Patia	Greek	intellectual woman
Patrice	Latin	bright, beautiful
Paula	Latin	small woman
Pax	Latin	peaceful, joyful
Paz	Arabic	golden one
Pearl	Latin	precious sea gem
Pegma	Greek	happy, content
Peace	Earth	finished, complete
Pelagia	Greek	sea woman
Pele	Island	from the volcano
Pelia	Hebrew	marvelous woman
Pelicia	Greek	weaving woman
Penda	African	loves, loved
Penelope	Greek	floating duck
Penina	Greek	humble
Peninnah	Hebrew	precious stone
Peony	Greek	colorful flower
Perla	Latin	tested, important
Perle	Latin	a pearl
Persephone	Greek	taken, strength
Persis	Greek	girl of the sea

Petrina	Latin	solid rock
Phebe	Greek	smiling girl
Phedra	Greek	brightness
Philana	Greek	lover of mankind
Philippa	Greek	lover of horses
Philomena	Greek	lover of strength
Phoebe	Greek	bright moon
Phoena	Greek	mystical bird
Phyllis	Greek	shrubbery, ferns
Pililani	Island	near to heaven
Polymnia	Greek	filled with song
Poni	African	second daughter
Poppy	Earth	orange, red flower
Pora	Hebrew	fertile woman
Portia	Latin	generous offering
Posy	Earth	small weeds, flowers
Praise	Latin	expresses admiration
Precia	Latin	important woman
Prilla	Celtic	small wild rose
Prisca	Latin	ancient family
Priscilla	Latin	ancient family
Pristina	Latin	unspoiled
Prosera	Latin	fortunate
Prova	Latin	provincial woman
Psyche	Greek	of the soul
Pua	Island	flower
Pules	Nat. Am.	pigeon
Puma	Latin	mountain lion

| Qadira | Arabic | capable, powerful |

Qamra	Arabic	of the moon
Qi	Asian	life force
Qiao	Asian	attractive girl
Quan	Asian	compassionate woman
Quana	Nat. Am.	sweet-smelling
Quartilla	Latin	fourth-born child
Quibila	Arabic	agreeable, pleasant
Quenby	Norse	feminine
Questa	Latin	a seeker
Quies	Latin	tranquility
Quilla	Incan	moon goddess
Quinlan	Celtic	strong and slender
Quintana	Latin	fifth daughter
Quintessa	Latin	of the essence
Quirina	Latin	protector, warrior girl
Quirita	Latin	loyal citizen
Quorra	Latin	from the heart

Rabab	Arabic	small cloud
Rabiah	Egyptian	gentle spring wind
Rachel	Hebrew	innocent lamb
Radha	Hindi	successful woman
Rafa	Arabic	happy, prosperous
Rafela	Hebrew	divine healer
Rahab	Hebrew	trustworthy
Raine	Earth	blessed from above
Raisa	Arabic	a leader
Raisel	Hebrew	a lovely rose
Raissa	Hebrew	rose, rosebud

Ranana	Hebrew	luscious
Rani	Hindi	queen
Rani	Hebrew	a singer
Rasha	Arabic	young gazelle
Rashida	Arabic	righteous direction
Ratana	Asian	a crystal
Raven	Earth	mysterious bird
Rayna	Norse	wise and pure
Raz	Hebrew	God's secret
Rebecca	Hebrew	bound to God
Regan	Celtic	royal-born
Regina	Latin	queenly
Rena	Hebrew	melody
Reneta	Latin	dignified
Reseda	Latin	mignonette flower
Reshma	Arabic	silky skin
Reumah	Hebrew	exalted woman
Reut	Hebrew	friend, fellowship
Rhan	Celtic	destiny
Rhea	Greek	flowing stream
Rhesa	Hebrew	affectionate woman
Rhoda	Greek	a soft red rose
Rhys	Celtic	enthusiasm, smiling
Rima	Arabic	white antelope
Rind	Norse	very large woman
Risa	Latin	one who laughs
Rita	Latin	child of light
River	Earth	flowing, connected
Rivka	Hebrew	to bind or fix
Rizpah	Greek	hope
Roe	Nat. Am.	female deer
Romney	Celtic	the source, strength
Ronat	Celtic	seal, fortitude
Rory	Celtic	red queen

Rosalba	Latin	white rose
Rose	Greek	meaningful flower
Roselani	Island	heavenly rose
Rosemary	Latin	dew of the sea
Rosetta	Latin	baby rose flower
Rosie	Latin	the rose
Rowa	Arabic	lovely vision
Roxane	Greek	star, bright dawn
Ruby	Earth	precious red gem
Ruhamah	Hebrew	beloved
Ruhani	Sanskrit	spiritual
Rukan	Arabic	confident, steadfast
Rumah	Hebrew	exalted woman
Rumina	Latin	protector
Runa	Norse	secret lore
Ruth	Hebrew	friend, companion
Ryo	Asian	excellence
Ryanne	Celtic	royal woman

Saba	Arabic	morning-born
Sabi	Arabic	lovely young woman
Sabirah	Arabic	patient, calm
Sacha	Greek	defender of all
Safa	Arabic	pure, innocent
Safia	African	lion's share
Saga	Norse	all seeing
Sagara	Hindi	ocean child
Sagira	Egyptian	little one
Sagit	Hebrew	sublime

Sahar	Arabic	of the dawn
Sahara	Arabic	of the desert
Sahirah	Egyptian	clean, perfect
Sakti	Hindi	divine energy
Saku	Asian	remembrance of God
Salma	Arabic	helmet of God
Salome	Hebrew	peace
Salwa	Arabic	provides comfort
Samala	Hebrew	requested of God
Samya	Arabic	exalted one
Sana	Arabic	brilliant
Sandrine	Greek	defender of men
Sanura	African	kitten-like
Sapphira	Arabic	beautiful gem
Sarah	Hebrew	princess
Sarahfina	Hebrew	angel, princess
Sarai	Hebrew	contentious
Saraid	Celtic	excellent, best
Saran	African	bringer of joy
Saree	Arabic	noble woman
Sarisha	Hindi	pleasant, charming
Sarki	African	chief or president
Sasa	Asian	helpful, caring
Sasha	Greek	defending men
Sason	Hebrew	bringer of joy
Sati	Hindi	truth-speaker
Satinka	Nat. Am.	magical dancer
Sato	Asian	sweet-natured
Saura	Hindi	of the heavens
Sebiya	Arabic	lovely girl
Seema	Greek	sign or symbol
Seirial	Celtic	bright
Seirian	Celtic	sparkling
Selah	Hebrew	rock-strong

Selda	Celtic	rare, precious
Selena	Greek	of the moon
Selma	Latin	divine protection
Sema	Arabic	divine symbol
Semine	Norse	sun, moon, stars
Semina	Hebrew	from heaven
Sena	Latin	blessed
Senga	Greek	pure, chaste
Sentia	Latin	children's guide
Seonaid	Celtic	gift of God
Sephora	Hebrew	beautiful bird
Sequoia	Nat. Am.	giant redwood, strong
Serah	Hebrew	abundance
Seraphina	Hebrew	heaven's angel
Serenity	Earth	peaceful
Sesheta	Egyptian	star goddess
Setu	Hindi	sacred symbol
Sevita	Hindi	cherished
Shada	Nat. Am.	sea bird
Shai	Celtic	gift of God
Shaina	Hebrew	beauty
Shakila	Arabic	beautiful one
Shalimar	Hindi	fragrant perfume
Shalva	Hebrew	protection
Shana	Hebrew	beautiful one
Shannon	Celtic	ancient wisdom
Shanti	Hindi	tranquil one
Sharon	Hebrew	plains flower
Shasta	Nat. Am.	snowy mountain
Shayleigh	Celtic	fairy princess
Sheerah	Hebrew	song, singer
Shelomith	Hebrew	peace, happiness
Shelomoth	Hebrew	peace, stability
Sherah	Aramaic	bright light

Shifra	Hebrew	child-bringer, beauty
Shiloh	Hebrew	peace, abundant
Shimeath	Hebrew	obedience
Shimrith	Hebrew	keeper, guard
Shiphrah	Hebrew	loveliness
Shir	Hebrew	meadow shire
Shira	Hebrew	joyous song
Shiran	Arabic	charming, sweet
Shirli	Hebrew	bright clearing
Shomer	Hebrew	guardian, watcher
Shona	Celtic	God is gracious
Shoshana	Arabic	graceful lily, white
Shu	Asian	gentle, kind, caring
Shua	Hebrew	daughter of opulence
Sian	Celtic	God is gracious
Sibyl	Celtic	bountiful, prophetess
Sidra	Latin	bright, starlike
Sienna	Latin	treasured, bronze
Signea	Latin	noble birthmark, sign
Sigrid	Norse	beautiful victory, advisor
Sika	African	prosperous woman
Silka	Latin	blind, perceptive
Silki	Norse	heavenly, drawn up
Silver	Earth	pale, sparkling treasure
Sima	Arabic	treasured prize
Simcha	Hebrew	joyous
Sina	Island	moon goddess
Sine	Hebrew	God is gracious
Sippora	Hebrew	birdlike woman
Sirena	Greek	beautiful, appealing
Sirine	Greek	beautiful singing
Sisay	African	blessing from God
Sisel	Norse	heavenly
Sita	Hindi	harvest goddess

Siv	Norse	beautiful bride
Sivan	Hebrew	springtime
Sky	Earth	from the heavens
Skye	Celtic	from the isle
Slama	Egyptian	peaceful one
Snow	Earth	white, shining
Sofia	Greek	wisdom
Solace	Latin	comfort
Solana	Latin	eastern breeze
Solaris	Greek	of the sun, warming
Solvig	Norse	strongest leader
Solne	Greek	wise, knowing
Sophia	Greek	wisdom, foresight
Sophronia	Greek	wise
Sora	Nat. Am.	chirping birds
Sorano	Asian	heavenly
Sorcha	Celtic	bright, a lady
Sparrow	Earth	songbird
Spika	Latin	bright star
Spirit	Earth	breath, life
Spring	Earth	springtime
Sroda	African	respected
Stacia	Latin	reborn
Star	Earth	celestial one
Stefania	Greek	laurel-leaf garland
Stefanie	Greek	victory crown
Stella	Latin	starlight, sea star
Stephanie	Greek	laurel garland
Stina	Norse	follows Christ
Storm	Earth	nature of a tempest
Subira	African	patient one
Sugar	Earth	sweet, island cane
Suha	Arabic	a star
Sukie	Asian	dearly loved

Sulleigh	Celtic	dark-eyed woman
Sultanna	Arabic	empress, ruler
Sumee	Asian	delicate flower
Summer	Earth	summer-born
Sunita	Hindi	well mannered
Sunshine	Earth	brilliant, cheerful
Suri	Sanskrit	mother of the sun
Susanna	Hebrew	graceful white lily
Suzu	Asian	one who lives long
Svea	Norse	motherland
Svenhilda	Norse	warrior woman, strong
Sweta	Hindi	bright, fair star
Synah	Greek	two together
Syntyche	Greek	fate, destiny

Taban	Celtic	brilliant genius
Tabia	Egyptian	talented
Tabita	African	graceful, silent
Tabitha	Greek	gazelle
Taborry	Nat. Am.	a voice that's heard
Tacita	Latin	silenced
Tahpenes	Hebrew	secret temptation
Tai	Asian	talented
Taisa	Greek	bond woman, servant
Tayma	Nat. Am.	loud thunder
Tal	Hebrew	morning dew
Talia	Greek	flourishing
Talitha	Aramaic	little girl
Talora	Hebrew	touch of morning dew

Tam	Asian	beloved
Tamar	Hebrew	date palm
Tamara	Sanskrit	a spice
Tamsin	Aramaic	a twin
Tamma	Hebrew	without flaw
Tansy	Greek	immortal
Tany	Asian	a sweetheart
Tapaty	Hindi	daughter of the sun
Tara	Celtic	high and rocky hill
Taryn	Celtic	high and earthen hill
Tarub	Arabic	happiness-bringer
Tava	Norse	staff of god
Tayen	Nat. Am.	birth at new moon
Teagan	Celtic	attractive girl
Tedra	Greek	supreme gift
Teigra	Greek	close to a tiger
Tekla	Greek	glory of God
Tellus	Latin	mother earth
Tema	Hebrew	righteous one
Terah	Latin	earth
Teresa	Greek	harvester
Tertia	Latin	third-born child
Tessa	Greek	harvester
Tevah	Hebrew	nature child
Thais	Greek	diadem
Thea	Greek	goddess
Thelma	Greek	ambitious
Theodora	Greek	gift of God
Theola	Greek	divine, godly
Thera	Greek	harvester
Therona	Greek	huntress
Thomasa	Hebrew	a twin
Thorberta	Norse	brilliance of Thor
Tia	Greek	royal daughter

Tiara	Latin	crowned one
Tieve	Celtic	from the hillside
Tiffany	Greek	manifestation of God
Tikva	Hebrew	hope
Tilly	Norse	mighty one
Timandra	Greek	daughter
Timna	Hebrew	respectful, protest
Timothea	Greek	to honor God
Tira	Hebrew	encampment
Tirza	Hebrew	pleasant, delight
Tisa	African	ninth-born child
Titania	Greek	giant, honored
Tiva	Nat. Am.	lover of dance
Toby	Hebrew	God is good
Toki	Asian	hopeful, resourceful
Tora	Norse	thunder
Torni	Norse	newly discovered
Torrin	Celtic	hill dancer
Tosca	Latin	volcanic Tuscany rock
Tosia	Latin	inestimable
Tova	Hebrew	well behaved
Tracie	Latin	brave woman
Tranquility	Latin	devout
Tree	Earth	tall, giving
Tressa	Celtic	long locks of hair
Trinity	Latin	threefold
Triveni	Hindi	three sacred rivers
True	Celtic	disciple, sincere
Tryphena	Greek	dainty, delicate
Tryphosa	Hebrew	soft, shine three times
Tuccia	Latin	vestal virgin
Tula	Hindi	balance
Tulsi	Hindi	a sacred plant
Tyra	Norse	justice

Tyro	Greek	fertile woman
Tziyone	Hebrew	woman of Zion
Tzipora	Hebrew	beauty, little bird

Udjit	Egyptian	snake tamer
Uchenna	African	God's will
Ujanna	African	a young woman
Ulalya	Greek	well spoken
Ulani	Island	cheerful one
Ulima	Arabic	astute, wise
Uma	Hindi	mother, sunlight
Una	Latin	unity, pure
Unice	Greek	conqueror
Unn	Norse	loved one
Unni	Hebrew	temple musician
Urbi	Egyptian	royal woman
Urenna	African	father's pride
Uri	Hebrew	light of the Lord
Uriana	Greek	heavenly
Uriela	Hebrew	angel of light
Urica	Nat. Am.	useful to all
Urit	Hebrew	to give off light
Ursula	Greek	small bear
Usha	Hindi	daughter of heaven
Ushir	Latin	mouth of the river
Uta	Asian	poetic, meaningful
Utas	Latin	glorious woman
Utasta	Arabic	of the homeland
Uzuri	African	deep beauty

| Uzi | Hebrew | God is my strength |

Vacuna	Latin	victorious woman
Vatilda	Norse	mother, helper
Vailea	Island	talking waters
Valida	Latin	brave, strong woman
Valine	Latin	vigor and health
Valentine	Latin	vigorous, healthy
Valara	Latin	strong, valiant
Valki	Norse	handmaiden
Valonia	Latin	from the valley
Vandani	Hindi	worthy, honorable
Vanessa	Greek	delicate butterfly
Vangy	Greek	bringer of good news
Vana	Asian	golden-haired
Vanthe	Greek	blonde woman
Vara	Greek	cautious
Varana	Hindi	of the river
Varda	Hebrew	rose
Varsha	Hindi	of the rain
Vashti	Arabic	lovely woman
Vassy	Arabic	pretty young woman
Vayu	Hindi	life force, oxygen
Veata	Asian	of the wind
Veda	Sanskrit	wisdom, knowledge
Vega	Latin	falling star
Venda	African	middle people
Venus	Greek	goddess of love, beauty
Venya	Hindi	lovable

Vera	Latin	truth
Verda	Latin	young, fresh, springlike
Vered	Hebrew	rose
Verity	Latin	truthful
Vesna	Slavic	messenger, springtime
Victoire	Latin	victorious woman
Vida	Latin	life
Vidia	Hindi	wisdom
Vigdis	Norse	goddess
Vilina	Hindi	dedicated
Vilmaris	Greek	sea-protector
Violet	Earth	purple flower
Vina	Hindi	musical, wisdom
Vinaya	Hindi	disciplined
Vincentia	Latin	triumph
Virginia	Latin	chaste, pure
Virgo	Latin	the virgin
Vita	Latin	life
Vivian	Latin	vibrant life
Voleta	Greek	veiled woman
Vor	Norse	omniscient goddess

Wafa	Arabic	faithful, devoted
Wakana	Asian	thriving woman
Waki	Nat. Am.	protected place
Walta	African	human shield
Wan	Asian	gentle, gracious
Waneta	Nat. Am.	shapeshifter
Wapeka	Nat. Am.	skillful, ambidextrous

Waqi	Arabic	swooping flight
Warda	Arabic	fragrant rose
Wei	Asian	brilliant, valuable
Weiko	Nat. Am.	beautiful girl
Wende	Teutonic	wanderer
Wenna	Latin	maiden
Wila	Greek	helmet, protection
Wileen	Teutonic	defender
Winda	African	great huntress
Wing	Asian	woman of glory
Winna	African	beloved friend
Winona	Nat. Am.	firstborn daughter
Wren	Earth	songbird
Wyn	Celtic	fair white wave
Wyss	Celtic	fair, a beauty

Xabrina	Latin	legendary princess
Xanadu	African	exotic paradise
Xandra	Greek	defender of all
Xanthe	Greek	blonde woman
Xara	Hebrew	princess
Xaviera	Arabic	bright, knowledgeable
Xena	Greek	welcoming woman
Xerena	Latin	sign, symbol
Xing	Asian	star
Xing Xing	Asian	twin stars
Xochiquetzal	Aztec	feathery flower
Xochitl	Nat. Am.	many-flowered place
Xola	African	stay in peace

Xue	Asian	woman of snow
Xylia	Greek	woodland dweller
Xylina	Greek	forest dweller
Xylona	Greek	from the woods

Yabel	Hebrew	lovable one
Yadira	Hebrew	beloved friend
Yael	Hebrew	strength of God
Yaffa	Hebrew	beautiful woman
Yair	Hebrew	God will teach
Yaki	Asian	tenacious woman
Yakira	Hebrew	dear to the heart
Yalena	Greek	shining light
Yama	Asian	from the mountain
Yamha	Arabic	like a dove
Yamilla	Arabic	beautiful woman
Yamin	Hebrew	right hand
Yamka	Nat. Am.	blossom
Yanna	Hebrew	he answers
Yancy	Nat. Am.	northern, spirited
Yannis	Hebrew	gift of God
Yaser	Arabic	prosperous woman
Yashira	Asian	blessed, grace
Yasmin	Arabic	fragrant jasmine
Ydel	Hebrew	one who praises
Yedida	Hebrew	beloved friend
Yei	Asian	thriving woman
Yehudit	Hebrew	tribe of Judah
Yepa	Nat. Am.	winter princess

Yerial	Hebrew	founded by God
Yessena	Arabic	flowerlike
Yeshi	African	thousandfold
Yessica	Hebrew	He sees
Yi	Asian	bringer of happiness
Yin	Asian	silvery woman
Yitta	Hebrew	emanating light
Yocheved	Hebrew	God's glory
Yoella	Hebrew	one who loves God
Yoki	Nat. Am.	of the rain
Yoko	Asian	good, positive, achiever
Yolanda	Greek	modest, violet flower
Yoli	Greek	violet flower
Yon	Asian	lotus flower
Yona	Hebrew	a soft dove
Yonina	Hebrew	little dove
Yordana	Hebrew	downriver
Yori	Asian	reliable, trustworthy
Yoshi	Asian	respectful girl
Yovela	Hebrew	full of joy
Yseult	Celtic	a fair monarch
Yu	Asian	jade gem, moonlight
Yuki	Asian	woman of the snow
Yumn	Arabic	successful
Yuna	African	outstanding girl
Yuri	Asian	lily flower
Yusra	Arabic	prosperous one
Yuta	Hebrew	praised one

| Zada | Arabic | blessed, prosperous |

Zafara	Hebrew	one who sings
Zahar	Hebrew	golden morning dawn
Zahia	Arabic	brilliant, lovely
Zaina	Arabic	beautiful woman
Zaria	Arabic	royal rose
Zaka	African	pure, chaste
Zale	Greek	strength of the sea
Zamara	Hebrew	a songstress
Zamella	African	works to succeed
Zan	Asian	supportive, kind
Zana	Hebrew	delicate white lily
Zandra	Greek	defender of all
Zane	Norse	bold one
Zanita	Hebrew	God's gracious gift
Zanta	African	beautiful young woman
Zanthe	Greek	blonde woman
Zara	Arabic	awakening dawn
Zarifa	Arabic	successful
Zarina	African	golden one
Zarmina	African	bright one
Zarna	Hindi	spring of water
Zaza	Hebrew	belonging to all
Zia	Latin	wheat field, grain
Zebina	Greek	gifted one
Zebudah	Hebrew	endowed, endowment
Zehira	Hebrew	protected one
Zela	Greek	blessed with happiness
Zelia	Greek	zeal, enthusiasm
Zemira	Hebrew	joyful melody
Zen	Greek	daughter of God, dove
Zena	African	great fame
Zenas	Greek	generous one
Zenia	Greek	welcoming
Zeptah	Egyptian	daughter of Ptaú Egypts

Zera	Hebrew	sower of seeds
Zeresh	Hebrew	brilliant, golden
Zeruiah	Hebrew	balm of God
Zeta	Greek	born last, youngest
Zeva	Hebrew	splendor
Zia	Arabic	emanates pure light
Zibiah	Hebrew	female deer, doe
Zillah	Hebrew	shaded one, shadow
Zilpah	Hebrew	frail, dignified
Zimra	Hebrew	songs of praise
Zina	African	a secret spirit
Zinaida	Greek	of Zeus
Zinerva	Celtic	fair, blonde
Zinnia	Latin	bright and fancy flower
Ziona	Hebrew	goodness, hope
Zipporah	Hebrew	beauty, small bird
Zira	African	path, route
Ziva	Hebrew	radiant and bright
Zoa	Greek	vibrant, full of life
Zoe	Greek	life-giving, alive
Zohara	Hebrew	emanating sparkles, light
Zola	African	tranquil woman
Zona	Latin	decorative belt, scarf
Zonta	Nat. Am.	an honest woman
Zosa	Greek	an energetic woman
Zula	African	brilliant one
Zuleikah	Arabic	brilliant, fair, lovely
Zulma	Arabic	vibrant one
Zuni	Nat. Am.	creative one
Zuri	African	lovely, white, pure
Zurial	Hebrew	Lord is my rock
Zweena	Arabic	beautiful one
Zwi	Norse	a flashing gazelle
Zylia	Greek	woodland dweller

the names
masculine

name	source	meaning
Aadesh	Hindi	command, order
Aanand	Sanskrit	happiness, bliss
Aaron	Hebrew	mountain
Aastik	Hindi	has faith in God
Abacuc	Latin	embrace
Abaddon	Hebrew	place of destruction
Abantes	Greek	ancient Ionian tribe
Abarron	Hebrew	father of a multitude
Abas	Arabic	father, simple or primitive
Abba	Arabic	father
Abdias	Hebrew	servant of God
Abe	Hebrew	father of many nations
Abednego	Arabic	servant of Nebo
Abel	Hebrew	breath
Abell	Hebrew	exhalation of breath
Abia	Hebrew	God is my father

Abiah	Hebrew	God is my father
Abidan	Hebrew	father of judgment
Abiel	Hebrew	God is my father
Abihu	Hebrew	He is my father
Abijah	Hebrew	God is my father
Abimael	Hebrew	my father is God
Abimelech	Hebrew	my father is king
Abinadi	Eblaite	my father is exalted
Abir	Hebrew	strong
Abiram	Hebrew	my father is exalted
Abisai	Island	gift from God
Abisha	Hebrew	the Lord is my father
Abishai	Hebrew	gift from God
Abner	Greek	my father is light
Abraam	Hebrew	father of multitudes
Abraham	Hebrew	father of nations
Abram	Hebrew	high father
Absalom	Hebrew	father of peace
Abyan	Arabic	clear, distinct
Achaicus	Greek	sorrowing, sad
Achaikos	Greek	from Achaia
Achak	Nat. Am.	spirit
Achal	Hindi	constant, immovable
Achan	Aramaic	change, trouble
Adalia	Hebrew	YAHWEH is just
Adam	Hebrew	earth, man
Adamu	Island	red earth
Adar	Hebrew	noble
Adarsh	Hindi	ideal
Addai	Hebrew	man of God
Adeela	Arabic	justice, equal
Aden	Gaelic	fire, attractive, handsome
Adin	Hebrew	slender
Adino	Hebrew	slender, adorned

Adlai	Hebrew	God is just
Adley	Hebrew	just
Admon	Hebrew	red peony
Adniel	Hebrew	of God's flock
Adon	Hebrew	Lord, master
Adonai	Hebrew	my Lord is my ruler
Adonijah	Hebrew	my Lord is YAHWEH
Adoniram	Hebrew	my Lord is exalted
Adriel	Hebrew	God's flock
Advay	Hindi	unique
Aegon	Greek	to do, act or govern
Aeson	Greek	healer
Aesop	Greek	a writer of fables
Aetes	Greek	of the sun god, son of Sol
Agathon	Greek	good
Agendra	Hindi	king of the mountains
Ageno	Greek	most brave
Ager	Latin	gatherer
Agetos	Celtic	messenger
Agis	Greek	kings of Greek myth
Agrias	Greek	Sanskrit sons of kings
Agrim	Hindi	first, leaders
Agrippa	Latin	born feet first, wild horse
Aha	Egyptian	brother
Ahab	Hebrew	father's brother, uncle
Ahah	Hebrew	brother of YAHWEH
Ahan	Hindi	of the nature of time itself
Ahanu	Nat. Am.	he laughs
Aharon	Hebrew	mountain of strength
Ahiga	Nat. Am.	he fights
Ahmik	Hebrew	strength of God's flock
Ahmik	Nat. Am.	beaver
Ahote	Nat. Am.	restless one
Ahsalom	Hebrew	father of peace

Aias	Greek	mourner
Aitan	Hebrew	strong
Aitan	African	fights for possession
Ajay	Hindi	unconquerable, invincible
Ajoy	Hindi	joyful
Akand	Hindi	calm
Akando	Nat. Am.	ambush
Akash	Hindi	sky
Akecheta	Nat. Am.	fighter
Akiba	Hebrew	heal, replaces
Akim	Hebrew	established by God
Akish	Hurrian	the sun god has given
Akish	Jaredite	a king, bringer of evil
Akiva	Hebrew	protect, heal, replaces
Aksel	Hebrew	peace, father
Akub	Hebrew	replaces
Akule	Nat. Am.	he looks up
Alak	Hindi	world, beautiful tresses
Alastor	Greek	avenger, defender of man
Alcon	Greek	falcon, hawk
Alexander	Greek	defender of men
Alexis	Greek	defender
Alijah	Hebrew	the Lord is my God
Alim	Arabic	wise, learned
Alketas	Greek	strength
Allon	Hebrew	oak
Alma	Hebrew	lad of God
Alma	Eblaite	merchant
Alo	Nat. Am.	spiritual guide
Aloeus	Greek	father of giants
Alok	Hindi	cry of triumph
Aloki	Hindi	brightness
Alon	Hebrew	oak tree
Alop	Hindi	does not disappear

Alphaeus	Hebrew	changing
Alphaios	Greek	changing
Alter	Hebrew	old
Altes	Greek	high, high musical note
Alva	Norse	elf
Alvah	Arabic	exalted
Alvan	Hebrew	sublime
Amaan	Arabic	protection, without fear
Amal	Hebrew	work, labor
Amaleki	Nephite	record-keeper
Amalickiah	Nephite	usurper, traitor
Aman	Arabic	security, trustworthy
Amani	African	peace
Amar	Arabic	immortal
Amaron	Arabic	moon
Amasa	Hebrew	burden
Ambar	Hindi	sky
Ambud	Hindi	cloud
Ameya	Hindi	boundless
Ami	Hebrew	my people
Amichai	Hebrew	my parents are alive
Amiel	Hebrew	God of my people
Amikam	Hebrew	rising nation
Amil	Hindi	invaluable, unattainable
Aminadab	Hebrew	my people are liberal
Aminadi	Nephite	translator, interpreter
Amir	Arabic	prince
Amir	Hebrew	treetop
Amiram	Hebrew	of lofty people
Amish	Hindi	honest
Amit	Hindi	friend
Amita	Hebrew	truth
Amiti	Hebrew	truth
Amittai	Hebrew	truth

Amlan	Hindi	unfading, forever bright
Amlici	Nephite	a dissenter, leader
Ammah	Nephite	missionary, his people
Ammaron	Nephite	record-keeper
Ammi	Hebrew	my people
Ammiel	Hebrew	God of my people
Ammitai	Hebrew	truth
Ammon	Egyptian	hidden
Ammoron	Nephite	traitor, king
Amnigaddah	Jaredite	king
Amnon	Hebrew	faithful
Amnor	Nephite	watchman, spy, coin
Amod	Hindi	delight, pleasure
Amon	Egyptian	hidden
Amoron	Hebrew	my nation is a joyful song
Amos	Hebrew	borne by God
Amram	Hebrew	exalted nation
Amulek	Nephite	missionary, teacher
Amulon	Eblaite	place name, unknown meaning
Amulon	Nephite	leader of priests of Noah
An	Asian	peace
Anah	Hebrew	answer
Anaiah	Hebrew	God has answered
Anan	Arabic	clouds
Anani	Hebrew	a cloud, prophecy, divination
Ananias	Hebrew	God is gracious
Anath	Hebrew	answer
Andrew	Greek	man, manly, warrior
Anek	Hindi	many
Ankur	Hindi	blossom, to sprout
Annas	Hebrew	gift of God, one who answers
Anoki	Nat. Am.	actor, pretender
Antaeus	Greek	mythical wrestler

Antenor	Latin	prior direction or path
Antiomno	Greek	without a name, unknown
Antionah	Greek	without anything, alone
Antionum	Greek	without a name, unknown
Antiphus	Greek	without light or knowledge
Aod	Celtic	mythical son of Lyr
Apenimon	Nat. Am.	worthy of trust
Apollo	Greek	destroyer
Aponivi	Nat. Am.	wind blows down the gap
Aquila	Latin	eagle, arrow
Aram	Hebrew	the highlands
Aran	Asian	forrest, woods
Aranck	Nat. Am.	star, stars
Aratus	Greek	from the didactic poet
Arcas	Greek	son who became Ursa Minor
Archan	Hindi	he worships
Archeantus	Nephite	a choice man
Archelaos	Greek	Macedonian king
Ardon	Hebrew	bronze
Areli	Hebrew	brave, heroic, lion
Argos	Greek	magnificent, shining
Ari	Hebrew	lion of God
Ariel	Hebrew	lion of God
Ariston	Greek	the best
Aristotle	Greek	the best purpose
Arlan	Norse	foreigner, noble's land
Aron	Hebrew	high mountain
Arshad	Arabic	pious, obedient, devout
Artemis	Greek	safe, contained
Arturas	Celtic	stone eagle, bear
Arvad	Hebrew	voyager, an exile
Arya	Sanskrit	great, noble, truthful
Asa	Hebrew	healer, physician
Asaf	Hebrew	gatherer

Asav	Sanskrit	lightening, sun, essence
Asher	Hebrew	blessed, happy, fortunate
Ashwin	Sanskrit	fortunate, swift
Asopus	Greek	mythical river god
Asphalion	Greek	lyric poet
Aster	Greek	star
Atalyah	Hebrew	afflicted of YAHWEH
Athira	Hebrew	trace, mark, record
Atma	Hindi	psyche, soul
Atman	Hindi	self
Atman	Nat. Am.	self
Atreus	Greek	father, king
Attalos	Greek	nourished
Atul	Hindi	no equal
Autonous	Greek	self-law
Avatar	Hindi	incarnation of god, descent
Avi	Hebrew	my father
Avidan	Hebrew	justice of God
Avidor	Hebrew	protector, genesis father
Aviel	Hebrew	my father, God
Avigdor	Hebrew	father, protector
Avihu	Hebrew	He is my father
Aviram	Hebrew	exalted
Avirat	Hindi	constant, continuous
Avisha	Hebrew	drawn up of God
Avital	Hebrew	father of dew
Avniel	Hebrew	my strength is in God
Avonaco	Nat. Am.	thin, small bear
Avram	Hebrew	father of nations
Awan	Nat. Am.	someone exceptional
Axel	Norse	father of peace
Azarel	Hebrew	God is my guide
Azel	Hebrew	reserved, noble
Azeus	Greek	horse, player

| Azriel | Hebrew | God is my salvation |

Baba	Egyptian	firstborn
Bacis	Greek	oracle
Balas	Latin	blaze, bright flame
Bali	Hindi	mighty warrior
Balius	Greek	multicolored
Baltasar	Aramaic	royal protector
Bama	Hebrew	son of prophesy
Bandhu	Hindi	friend
Baqir	Arabic	great knowledge
Barak	Arabic	blessing
Baram	Hebrew	son of the nation
Bardas	Greek	mountain ridge
Barid	Hindi	cloud
Barnabas	Hebrew	son of comfort
Baron	Latin	man, freeman
Bart	Hebrew	plowman
Bartel	Hebrew	son of a farmer
Bartholomew	Aramaic	apostle, son of Tamai
Bartley	Earth	birch bark
Barukh	Hebrew	blessed
Barun	Hindi	lord of the sea
Bas	Celtic	fair-headed, spear
Basel	Greek	brave, courageous
Beelzebub	Hebrew	lord of flies, demon prince
Bela	Hebrew	God's oath within
Belshazzar	Hebrew	protected, last king
Ben	Hebrew	son of God's right hand

Benaiah	Hebrew	God has built
Benayahu	Hebrew	God builds
Bendis	Greek	well-pruned, moon
Benedict	Latin	blessed
Benedictson	Hebrew	son of Benedict
Benjamin	Hebrew	son of God's right hand
Benoni	Hebrew	son of my sorrow
Benroy	Hebrew	son of a lion
Bensen	Hebrew	son of Benedict
Benson	Island	excellent son
Benzion	Hebrew	son of Zion
Berakhiah	Hebrew	God blesses
Berengar	Celtic	spear of a bear
Bethuel	Hebrew	man of God
Betzalel	Hebrew	shadow of God
Beulah	Hebrew	promised land
Bianor	Greek	double suns
Bias	Greek	strong force
Bidziil	Nat. Am.	he is strong
Bilagaana	Nat. Am.	fair, white
Bilva	Hindi	sacred leaf
Bimal	Sanskrit	sacred leaf
Bimisi	Nat. Am.	slippery
Binah	Hebrew	wise
Bion	Greek	life
Bipin	Hindi	forest
Bir	Hindi	courageous
Biton	Greek	born after a long wait
Boas	Hebrew	swift
Boaz	Hebrew	strength, swiftness
Bodaway	Nat. Am.	maker of fire
Bogdan	Slavic	gift of God
Booz	Hebrew	swift, strong
Borak	Arabic	lightning

Boris	Slavic	battle glory
Boter	Greek	small fishing vessel
Brent	Hindi	hilltop
Brigham	Old English	bridge dwelling
Brison	Greek	sound of sleep
Bucoli	Latin	cheek balm, oil
Buz	Hebrew	seventh generation

Caiaphas	Greek	to raise up
Cainan	Latin	fixed
Cale	Celtic	bending reed
Caleb	Hebrew	devotion, faith
Calum	Latin	dove of peace
Canaan	Hebrew	land of reeds
Candelario	Latin	candlelight
Carmel	Hebrew	garden, vineyard
Carmelo	Hebrew	orchard, garden
Carmine	Hebrew	vineyard, orchard
Carpus	Greek	fruitful
Castor	Greek	beaver
Ceas	Greek	treasure box
Cephas	Hebrew	rock
Ceyx	Greek	beloved husband
Cezoram	Hebrew	governor, chief protector
Chagai	Hebrew	celebrate, mediate
Chaim	Hebrew	life
Chain	African	weaving leaf
Chalcon	Greek	small lizard, swift
Chaleb	Hebrew	faith, devotion

Chanan	Hebrew	gracious
Chananyah	Hebrew	compassion of God
Chander	Hindi	to shine as the moon
Chandrak	Hindi	lunar shining
Chandran	Hindi	bright moon shining
Chan	Asian	shining
Chane	African	weaving leaves
Chanoch	Hebrew	dedicated, initiated
Charan	Sanskrit	the feet of God
Charak	Asian	wandering scholar, doctor
Charles	Anglo-Saxon	free, manly
Charmides	Greek	temperance, heritage
Charon	Greek	fierce brightness
Charopos	Greek	bright-eyed, strong
Chatura	Hindi	skillful
Chavaqquq	Hebrew	embrace
Chaviv	Hebrew	beloved
Chayim	Hebrew	life
Chayton	Nat. Am.	falcon
Che	Gaelic	admirable
Chechi	Hindi	poetry
Cheiron	Greek	a wise centaur
Chemish	Egyptian	near Euphrates
Chenaniah	Hebrew	God establishes, music
Chepe	Hebrew	God will multiply
Chersis	Greek	cherry blossom, to fly
Chesmu	Nat. Am.	grit, grain
Chetan	Hindi	to exist, living
Cheveyo	Nat. Am.	ogre of Hopi folklore
Chi	Asian	youthful energy
Chilon	Greek	advisor, sage
Chiman	Hindi	curious
Chimon	Asian	wisdom gate
Chinar	Hindi	long-lived tree

Chintak	Sanskrit	thoughtful
Chiram	Hebrew	exalted
Chizqiyahu	Hebrew	fair, blond
Chochmo	Nat. Am.	mud mound
Chogan	Nat. Am.	blackbird
Choni	Hebrew	gracious
Choovio	Nat. Am.	antelope
Christ	Greek	Anointed One
Chromis	Greek	color, shine
Chronos	Greek	time
Chuchip	Nat. Am.	deer spirit
Cilix	Greece	drinking cup
Cineas	Greek	eidetic memory
Ciqala	Nat. Am.	little one
Clay	Old English	clay, river-earth
Cle	Celtic	clay, river-earth
Cleades	Greek	advisor
Cleon	Greek	good, glorious
Cleopas	Greek	son of a renowned father
Cleophas	Aramaic	friend of the Lord
Clinias	Greek	a wealthy captain
Clytius	Greek	mortal man
Cobon	Hebrew	following after
Cochise	Nat. Am.	hardwood, stoic
Codros	Greek	most honored sacrifice
Cohen	Hebrew	priest, high priest
Cohor	Hebrew	to bind together
Com	Latin	to connect
Conon	Celtic	swift-footed
Conn	Gaelic	chief
Conway	Gaelic	watchful, holy river
Coriantumr	Egyptian	enthroned king, of Atum
Corihor	Egyptian	prince, beloved of Horus
Cornelius	Latin	horn

Corom	Latin	crown
Corydon	Gaelic	spear
Crescens	Latin	increasing
Crios	Greek	ice, frozen
Cronos	Greek	a crow
Cumenihah	Nephite	commander
Cylon	Greek	youthful
Cyniscus	Greek	logician, theorist
Cyrus	Greek	master, lord

Dabi	Hebrew	beloved
Daetor	Greek	student of Troy
Dagan	Hebrew	grain, of earth
Dagon	Aramaic	Canaanite God
Daikan	Asian	great contemplation
Dainin	Asian	patience, endurance
Dakota	Nat. Am.	friends, allies
Dalit	Hindi	untouchable
Dallin	English	from the dale or valley
Daman	Celtic	to gentle or tame
Damian	Greek	to tame
Damon	English	to tame
Dan	Hebrew	to judge
Dana	Hebrew	arbiter
Danan	Island	volcano
Danaus	Greek	father of daughters
Dane	Celtic	Kingdom of Denmark
Danel	Hebrew	God judges
Danell	Hebrew	God is my judge

Dani	Indonesian	tribesmen
Daniel	Hebrew	God is my judge
Danihel	Latin	Roman prophet
Daniilu	Hebrew	God is my judge
Danil	Hebrew	God judges
Danish	Persian	wisdom, discernment
Daniyyel	Hebrew	God is our judge
Dann	Anglo-Saxon	valley dweller
Dannie	Hebrew	God judges
Dannon	Hebrew	God is my judge
Dantrell	Hebrew	God is my judge
Danyl	Hebrew	God is my judge
Daphis	Greek	laurel leaf
Dar	Hebrew	pearl
Dareios	Greek	cared for, well
Darius	Greek	maintains goods well
Daryawesh	Hebrew	to possess well
Dat	Asian	accomplished
Dathan	Hebrew	fountain
Datta	Sanskrit	given, gift
Dauid	African	favorite
Dave	Hebrew	beloved
Davi	Hebrew	beloved
David	Hebrew	beloved
Davidu	Slavic	beloved
Davin	Norse	beloved
Davos	Greek	beloved
Davu	African	beginning
Dawar	Arabic	wanderer
Dawid	Hebrew	beloved
Daya	Hindi	kind man
De	Asian	royal-born
Deacon	Greek	servant
Decimus	Latin	tenth-born

Deen	Anglo-Saxon	church official
Deep	Sanskrit	light, lamp
Deepak	Hindi	little lamp
Dekel	Hebrew	a palm date
Delaiah	Hebrew	freed by God
Delayahu	Hebrew	YAHWEH has drawn
Delius	Greek	man from Delos
Delphin	Greek	dolphin-like
Delsin	Nat. Am.	as he is, complete
Demades	Greek	after his father
Demothi	Nat. Am.	talks while walking
Dennis	Latin	follower of Dionysus
Deo	Greek	a goodly man
Deon	Greek	converted by Paul
Deron	Celtic	great, vast
Devadas	Hindi	servant of the Gods
Dev	Hindi	a kingly man
Devak	Hindi	a divine man
Devlin	Celtic	fiercely brave
Devrat	Hindi	divine feet
Devsena	Hindi	army of gods
Dexios	Greek	two, twice, twins
Dexter	Latin	skilled, right-handed
Dia	African	champion
Dien	Asian	farmer
Dicaeus	Greek	son of the sea
Dichali	Nat. Am.	he who speaks a lot
Digant	Hindi	horizon, skyline
Digby	Norse	near the ditch, a digger
Diji	African	a farmer
Dilip	Hindi	royal one
Diklah	Aramaic	date tree
Dilber	Hindi	one who loves
Dillon	Celtic	faithful, lionlike man

Din	African	a prodigious man
Dinar	Hindi	gold coin
Dinesh	Hindi	of the sun
Dinos	Greek	steadfast and firm
Diocles	Greek	glory of God
Dobi	African	one who cleans clothing
Dohosan	Nat. Am.	a small bluff
Dolon	Celtic	dark-haired
Dominic	Latin	a lord
Domnall	Gaelic	world ruler
Donagh	Celtic	brown-haired, strong
Donar	Teutonic	god of thunder
Dor	Hebrew	a generation, home
Doren	Celtic	dweller, gift
Dorian	Greek	gift
Dorsea	Gaelic	fortress near the sea
Dosney	Celtic	from the sandy hill
Dost	Arabic	beloved friend
Dotan	African	hardworking man
Dov	Hebrew	a whisper
Dovev	Hebrew	a bear
Doyal	Gaelic	a dark stranger
Drew	Celtic	wise one
Driscol	Celtic	mediator, messenger
Dron	Hindi	teacher, instructor
Dryas	Greek	oak tree
Duane	Gaelic	tawny man
Dugal	Celtic	dark stranger
Due	Asian	a virtuous man
Duer	Celtic	a heroic man
Dugan	Gaelic	a swarthy man
Dumea	African	like a bull
Dunbar	Gaelic	headland castle
Dunham	Celtic	brown-haired man

Dunn	Gaelic	brown-haired warrior
Durand	Latin	an enduring man
Durbin	Latin	dwells near the city
Durga	Hindi	the unreachable
Duris	Greek	imperfect ruler
Dyami	Nat. Am.	like an eagle
Dylyn	Celtic	son of the sea
Dymas	Greek	mythological father

Ean	Gaelic	God is gracious
Eban	Hebrew	solid as a rock
Ebenezer	Hebrew	rock of help
Ebrahim	Arabic	father of nations
Echo	Greek	a sound returned
Edan	Celtic	full of fire
Eden	Hebrew	pleasure garden
Eder	Hebrew	of the flock
Edi	African	treasure-keeper
Edom	Hebrew	red-haired man
Edrian	Latin	man of Hadria
Efraim	Latin	a productive man
Efrat	Hebrew	honored
Efron	Hebrew	songbird
Ehud	Hebrew	united
Eilad	Hebrew	God is eternal
Eilif	Norse	immortal
Einar	Norse	chief warrior
Eiran	Gaelic	island
Eisa	Arabic	God is my salvation

Eisig	Hebrew	one who often laughs
Eitan	Hebrew	strong, firm, eager
Eka	Sanskrit	one
Ekani	Hindi	one, first
Eko	Indonesian	first child
Ekon	African	strong
Ekram	Hindi	honored man
Elan	Hebrew	oak tree
Elazar	Hebrew	God is my help
Eldad	Hebrew	beloved of God
Eleazar	Hebrew	God has helped
Eleon	Greek	victorious
Elhanan	Hebrew	God is gracious
Eli	Hebrew	high, ascended
Eliam	Hebrew	God of my nation
Eliakim	Hebrew	God will establish
Elias	Latin	my Lord is God
Eliezer	Hebrew	God is my help
Elihu	Hebrew	He is my God
Elijah	Hebrew	my God is Lord
Elim	Hebrew	from the oasis
Elimu	African	scientific knowledge
Elioenai	Hebrew	my eyes toward God
Eliot	Hebrew	my God has helped
Eliou	Hebrew	my God is YAHWEH
Eliphelet	Hebrew	God is release
Eliron	Hebrew	my God is my song
Elisaie	Greek	my God is my salvation
Elisha	Hebrew	God is my salvation
Elishama	Hebrew	whom God hears
Eliud	Greek	God is great
Eliyyahu	Hebrew	the Lord is my God
Eljah	Hebrew	my God is the Lord
Elkanah	Hebrew	one who belongs to God

Ellis	Hebrew	Jehovah is my God
Elnathan	Hebrew	gift of God
Elne	Anglo-Saxon	a courageous man
Elon	Hebrew	oak tree
Elrad	Hebrew	God is the ruler
Elsu	Nat. Am.	a flying falcon
Elvys	Norse	one who is wise
Elwyn	Gaelic	fair, white, holy
Ely	Hebrew	my God on high
Emil	Latin	industrious, eager
Emanuel	Hebrew	God is with us
Emer	Arabic	a ruler, a prince
Emran	Arabic	exalted
Emron	Nephite	a soldier
Enapay	Nat. Am.	brave appearance
Endios	Greek	to wander, on God
Enoch	Hebrew	dedicated to God
Enops	Greek	a shepherd
Enos	Hebrew	man
Enosh	Hebrew	man
Ensign	Latin	banner, flag, symbol
Enyeto	Nat. Am.	walks like a bear
Eos	Greek	dawn-bringer
Epaphras	Hebrew	handsome, charming
Epeius	Greek	maker of the Trojan horse
Ephraim	Hebrew	fruitful, productive
Epicurus	Greek	enjoys life, pleasure
Eran	Hebrew	alert, watchful
Erasmus	Greek	one dearly loved
Erasto	African	peaceful man
Erastos	Greek	love
Eren	Hebrew	red earth
Eri	Hebrew	watchful protector
Eric	Norse	eternal ruler

Eron	Hebrew	exalted one
Eros	Greek	god of love
Esaias	Hebrew	God is my salvation
Esam	Arabic	safeguard
Esau	Hebrew	hairy man, twin
Esben	Norse	of God
Esdras	Greek	aid-giver
Eshkol	Hebrew	grape cluster
Eskel	Norse	from the gods cauldron
Esra	Hebrew	helper
Esrom	Hebrew	dart of joy, song break
Estes	Latin	lives near estuary
Etan	Hebrew	strong, firm, steadfast
Etchemin	Nat. Am.	canoe man
Ethan	Hebrew	firm and steadfast
Ether	Greek	surrounding air, firmament
Ether	Hebrew	left mark, trace, record
Ettan	Sanskrit	breath
Etu	Nat. Am.	of the sun
Eudoxus	Greek	honored opinion
Eugenius	Greek	wellborn man
Euphorion	Greek	abundant
Euripides	Greek	well thrown, composed
Eustace	Greek	abundance of grapes
Eutychos	Greek	well fated, blessed
Evenus	Greek	river-god
Evios	Greek	attributed to sound
Ewan	Gaelic	little swift one
Eyal	Hebrew	having great strength
Eyou	Hebrew	a symbol of piety
Ezar	Hebrew	one who offers assistance
Eze	African	a king
Ezechias	Latin	strengthen, fortify
Ezechiel	Hebrew	whom God strengthens

Ezekias	Greek	God will strengthen
Ezekiel	Hebrew	God will strengthen
Ezer	Hebrew	to aid, assist
Ezias	Hebrew	Old Testament prophet
Ezno	Nat. Am.	one who walks alone
Ezra	Hebrew	a helper

Fabio	Latin	a bean
Fadi	Arabic	a savior
Fahim	African	a scholar
Fai	Asian	of the beginning, light
Faizal	Arabic	decisive, resolute
Faizun	Arabic	understanding man
Falco	Latin	the falcon master
Faelin	Gaelic	little wolf
Farid	Arabic	unequaled
Farouk	Arabic	one who knows the truth
Faste	Norse	firm, unchanging one
Fatin	Arabic	intelligent man
Faust	Latin	blessed
Favien	Latin	full of wisdom
Faxon	Latin	thick and long hair
Feechi	African	one who worships God
Feige	Hebrew	birdlike
Feivel	Hebrew	brilliant one
Felim	Celtic	always good, gracious
Felix	Latin	happy, prosperous
Fenris	Norse	giant wolf
Fenton	English	marshlands

Feo	Nat. Am.	a confident man
Feoris	Gaelic	like a smooth rock
Ferdinand	German	courageous sailor
Fergael	Gaelic	strong, brave
Fergus	Gaelic	top and first choice
Ferron	Arabic	a baker
Festus	Latin	festive, joyous man
Fews	Celtic	from the woods
Fidelo	Latin	faithful
Fielding	English	from the field
Filippu	Greek	horse lover
Fineas	Egyptian	dark-skinned man
Finlay	Gaelic	fair-haired hero
Finn	Gaelic	fair-haired man
Firdus	Hindi	from paradise
Flavian	Latin	a blond man
Foley	English	a creative man
Foma	Hebrew	one of twins
Forbes	Gaelic	from the field
Ford	English	from a river crossing
Forrest	English	from the woodland
Fortney	Latin	great strength
Foy	Celtic	adventurous journey
Franz	Latin	a free man
Frederick	German	a peaceful ruler
Frey	Norse	god of peace
Frode	Norse	a wise man
Froyim	Hebrew	a kind man
Fudayle	Arabic	high moral character
Fyrsyl	Celtic	the staff-bearer

Gabai	Hebrew	a delightful man
Gabe	Hebrew	a hero of God
Gabor	Hebrew	God is my strength
Gabrian	Hebrew	God's able-bodied
Gabriel	Hebrew	a hero of God
Gad	Hebrew	has good fortune
Gad	Nat. Am.	of the juniper plant
Gadiel	Arabic	God is my fortune
Gadianton	Arabic/Latin	God is worthy
Gadish	Arabic	a shock of corn
Gair	Gaelic	man of short stature
Gal	Hebrew	rolling wave
Galahad	Celtic	summer hawk, strong
Galenus	Latin	blue-eyed man
Galen	Greek	a calm healer
Gali	Hebrew	from a fountain
Gallus	Hebrew	reckless, bold
Gallager	Gaelic	eager to help others
Gamaliel	Hebrew	God's reward
Gamil	Arabic	handsome man
Gan	Asian	a wanderer
Ganit	Hebrew	defender
Gannan	Gaelic	fair-skinned man
Garud	Hindi	starship, eagle
Gavi	Hebrew	God is my strength
Gavriel	Hebrew	God is my strength
Gavriilu	Hebrew	strong man for God
Gayan	Hindi	sky
Gazali	African	mystic, a gazer

Gedaliah	Hebrew	God is great
Gedeon	Hebrew	one who cuts, harvests
Geet	Hindi	song, ballad
Gefen	Hebrew	of the vine
Geirleif	Norse	son of the spear-maker
Geleon	Greek	son of Ion, Athens quarter
Gemariah	Hebrew	the Lord has perfected
Gemaryahu	Hebrew	accomplished, scribe's son
Genan	Asian	servant
Genaro	Latin	dedicated man
Gera	Latin	brother
Geremia	Latin	exalted by the Lord
Gersham	Hebrew	exiled, absence
Gershon	Hebrew	tabernacle-sojourner
Ghason	Arabic	the prime of youth
Ghedi	African	traveler
Giacomo	Latin	supplanter
Gian	Latin	God is gracious
Giannes	Latin	God is gracious
Gid	Hebrew	warrior, tree feller
Giddonah	Nephite	descendant, father
Gideon	Hebrew	hewer, powerful warrior
Gidgiddonah	Nephite	commander of ten thousand
Gidgiddoni	Nephite	prophet, commander
Gidon	Hebrew	warrior, tree feller
Gil	Hebrew	joy of the people
Gil	Gaelic	servant
Gilad	Hebrew	from the monument
Gilam	Hebrew	joy of the people
Gilby	Norse	from the hostage's estate
Gilgal	Hebrew	roll, dazzle, trust the Lord
Gilgamesh	Sumerian	antediluvian giant
Gilgamos	Greek	once and future king
Gilli	Gaelic	servant

Gilon	Hebrew	filled with joy
Ginton	Arabic	from the garden
Giovanni	Latin	God is gracious
Girvan	Gaelic	small, rough, gritty
Gitel	Hebrew	good, kind man
Givon	Arabic	from the high places
Gjord	Norse	God is peace
Glennon	Gaelic	of the glen
Godana	African	male child
Goel	Hebrew	redeemed
Gogo	African	grandfatherly
Goku	Asian	from the sky
Goliath	Hebrew	exiled, tall
Gomda	Nat. Am.	of the wind
Gomer	Hebrew	vanish, to complete, end
Gordias	Greek	farmer
Gordon	Celtic	hero from the hill
Goren	Hebrew	from the granary
Gorgos	Greek	terrible, dreadful
Gosheven	Nat. Am.	one who leaps or jumps
Gozal	Hebrew	baby bird
Gregorius	Greek	watchful, vigilant
Griffin	Latin	having a hooked nose
Gryllus	Greek	foreign voice
Gulzar	Arabic	garden of roses
Gunin	Hindi	virtuous
Gur	Hebrew	lion cub
Guri	Hebrew	plentiful
Gurion	Hebrew	son of the lion
Gus	Latin	majestic, exalted
Gustave	Norse	staff of the gods
Guy	Celtic	runner in the wood
Guyapi	Nat. Am.	open, honest, truth
Gwyn	Celtic	fair, handsome man

Gyan	Hindi	knowledge, intelligence
Gyras	Greek	reed
Gyth	Greek	positioning, direction

Habacuc	Hebrew	embrace, hug
Habib	Arabic	dearly loved
Hadar	Hebrew	respected, glorious
Haden	Celtic	heather hill
Hadi	Arabic	guide on the right path
Hadriel	Hebrew	splendor of God
Hagar	Hebrew	a wanderer
Hagen	Gaelic	youthful
Haggai	Hebrew	festive
Hagnon	Greek	holy, pure
Hagoth	Egyptian	warrior
Hakon	Norse	exalted, chosen race
Halen	Norse	hall of light
Halig	Anglo-Saxon	holy man
Halim	Arabic	a gentle man
Halius	Greek	youthful, exuberant
Halla	African	unexpected gift
Halle	Norse	solid as a rock
Halley	English	hall near the meadow
Hallwell	English	from the holy spring
Halvard	Norse	guardian of the rock
Ham	Hebrew	one who produces heat
Hamal	Arabic	resembling a lamb
Hamar	Norse	hammer-wielder
Hamden	Arabic	praised

Hamon	Norse	great leader
Hana	Hebrew	grace, favor
Hanan	Hebrew	of God's grace
Hanani	Arabic	merciful
Hananiah	Hebrew	YAHWEH is gracious
Hania	Nat. Am.	spirit warrior
Hanna	Arabic	God is gracious
Hannibal	Hebrew	the grace of Baal
Hans	Norse	God is gracious
Haran	Hebrew	mountaineer
Harel	Hebrew	mountain of God
Hari	Hindi	lion
Harim	Arabic	superior man
Harith	African	cultivator
Haroon	Arabic	mountain
Harrell	Hebrew	God's mountain
Harrod	Hebrew	heroic man, king
Haruni	African	a mountaineer
Hashim	Arabic	destroyer of evil
Hastiin	Nat. Am.	a man
Hastin	Hindi	like an elephant
Hatim	Arabic	determined, judge
Havilah	Hebrew	sacred circle, sand
Hazael	Hebrew	whom God beholds
Hearthom	Jaredite	middle son
Heber	Hebrew	companion, partner
Heer	Hindi	diamond
Hei	Asian	of grace
Hekli	Nat. Am.	touch
Helaku	Nat. Am.	born on a sunny day
Helam	Nephite	light
Helaman	Nephite	light
Helem	Nephite	light
Helge	Norse	productive, happy

Heli	Hebrew	offers himself to God
Helias	Greek	shining light, son of sun
Helmuth	Germanic	spirit and courage
Helorum	Nephite	knowledge, learning
Hem	Hindi	golden sun
Hem	Jaredite	unknown
Heman	Hebrew	faithful man
Hermes	Greek	messenger
Hero	Greek	brave defender
Herod	Hebrew	hero's ode, song
Herodes	Greek	hero's ode, song
Herodion	Hebrew	hero's ode, song
Herodotus	Greek	father of history
Herschel	Hebrew	deer
Hesutu	Nat. Am.	high insect nest
Hetal	Hindi	warm hearted
Heth	Jaredite	unknown
Hevel	Hebrew	breath, life source
Hezekiah	Hebrew	God is my strength
Hieremias	Hebrew	God will uplift
Hiero	Irish	saint name
Hieu	Asian	a pious man
Hiezecihel	Latin	God strengthens
Hillel	Hebrew	one who is praised
Himesh	Hindi	snow king
Himni	Nephite	son of Mosiah
Hinto	Nat. Am.	the color blue
Hippon	Greek	horse people
Hirah	Hebrew	noble, nobility
Hiram	Hebrew	highborn, whiteness
Hizkiah	Hebrew	son of Zechariah
Hod	Hebrew	glory
Hogen	Gaelic	youthful one
Honani	Nat. Am.	a badger

Honaw	Nat. Am.	a bear
Honi	Hebrew	a gracious man
Honon	Nat. Am.	a bear
Honovi	Nat. Am.	great strength
Horus	Egyptian	god of light
Hosea	Hebrew	to reach salvation
Hoshi	Asian	star
Hosni	Arabic	a superior man
Hotah	Nat. Am.	white hair and skin
Hototo	Nat. Am.	singing, whistling spirit
Howi	Nat. Am.	a turtledove
Huri	Hebrew	linen-weaver
Huritt	Nat. Am.	a handsome man
Hylas	Greek	mythical son
Hyllos	Greek	mythical one
Hyman	Hebrew	giver of life

Ian	Gaelic	God is gracious
Iachin	Latin	high, noble
Iacobus	Hebrew	supplanter
Iafeth	Latin	enlarged
Iair	Latin	he shines
Iairos	Greek	he shines
Iakobos	Greek	supplanter
Iakovos	Hebrew	supplanter, by heel
Iakovu	Old Slavic	may God protect
Iamus	Greek	unknown
Iaokim	Hebrew	God will establish

Iapheth	Nordic	handsome
Iared	Hebrew	descent
Iason	Greek	healer, to heal
Iasos	Greek	he will add
Icarion	Greek	mythic son of Daedalus
Icarus	Greek	winged man, son of Daedalus
Ichabod	Hebrew	without glory, humble
Idas	Greek	mythical argonaut
Iephthae	Greek	he opens
Ieremias	Greek	YAHWEH has uplifted
Iesous	Greek	YAHWEH is salvation
Iesus	Latin	Latin form of Jesus
Iezekiel	Greek	Greek form of Ezekiel
Igasho	Nat. Am.	he wanders, wanderer
Ike	English	from Hebrew Isaac, he laughs
Ilia	Russian	Hebrew of Elijah
Ilias	Latin	from Greek of Elias
Ilus	Latin	founder of Troy
Immanuel	Greek	within me is God
Inazin	Nat. Am.	standing elk
Ioan	Romanian	form of John, gracious
Ioannes	Greek	God is gracious
Iob	Greek	patient, persecuted
Iohel	Latin	YAHWEH is God
Ion	Greek	son of Apollo
Iona	Latin	dove
Ionnes	Hebrew	God is gracious
Ioram	Latin	exalted
Ioseph	Greek	he will add
Iosias	Latin	he will support
Iosue	Latin	YAHWEH is salvation
Iou	Greek	YAHWEH is He
Ioubal	Greek	stream

Ioudas	Greek	praised
Iov	Hebrew	God will establish
Ira	Hebrew	vigilant, watchful
Iram	Hebrew	shining man
Irfan	Arabic	thankful
Isaac	Hebrew	full of laughter
Isaakios	Greek	founder
Isaiah	Hebrew	God is my salvation
Isaias	Hebrew	God is my salvation
Isam	Arabic	protected, blessed
Isas	Asian	worthwhile
Iseabail	Hebrew	devoted to God
Ishaan	Hindi	of the sun
Ishaq	Arabic	laughing child
Ishi	Asian	solid, rock
Ishmael	Hebrew	God listens
Ishmerai	Hebrew	YAHWEH guards
Ishvi	Hebrew	He resembles me
Isiah	Hebrew	YAHWEH is salvation
Isidor	Greek	gift of Isis
Ismael	Latin	God will hear
Israel	Hebrew	God perseveres
Issa	Hebrew	gift of God
Issachar	Hebrew	He will reward
Issay	African	hairy one
Istaqa	Nat. Am.	coyote man
Istu	Nat. Am.	sugar sweet
Itai	Hebrew	God beside me
Itamar	Hebrew	from isle of palms
Ithai	Hebrew	with me
Ithiel	Hebrew	God with me
Ittai	Hebrew	He is with me
Itylus	Latin	of Italy
Iuwine	Latin	beloved friend

Ivrit	Hebrew	Hebrew language
Iyar	Hebrew	surrounded by light
Iye	Nat. Am.	of the smoke
Izaan	Arabic	obedient
Izzy	Hebrew	God contended

Ja	African	magnetic
Jaala	Hebrew	wild goat
Jaap	Hebrew	supplanter
Jaasau	Hebrew	they will do
Jabez	Hebrew	delivered in pain
Jabin	Hebrew	perceptive
Jabir	Arabic	provider of comfort
Jacan	Hebrew	troublemaker, funny
Jack	English	God is gracious
Jackal	Sanskrit	wild dog
Jacob	Hebrew	supplanter
Jacom	Hebrew	established by God
Jacot	Hebrew	supplanter
Jacy	English	God is gracious
Jad	Hebrew	benevolent
Jada	Latin	green gemstone
Jadon	Hebrew	thankful
Jael	Arabic	he who ascends
Jafar	Arabic	stream
Jagan	Hindi	universe, universal
Jagger	English	carrier of provisions, food
Jahan	Hindi	man of the world, universe
Jaime	Spanish	supplanter

Jair	Hebrew	God enlightens
Jaira	Hebrew	he will light up
Jairus	Hebrew	God enlightens
Jake	English	supplanter
Jakeem	Arabic	exalted one
Jakome	Basque	supplanter
Jal	English	wanderer
Jalal	Arabic	superior
Jaleel	Arabic	majestic
Jamal	Arabic	handsome
James	Hebrew	supplanter
Jamian	Hebrew	favored
Jamie	Hebrew	supplanter
Jamiel	Hebrew	right hand
Jamon	Hebrew	favored
Jan	Norse	God is gracious
Jani	Finnish	God is gracious
Jankia	Hebrew	gift of God
Janko	Hebrew	gift of God
Jannes	Norse	gift of God
Jantje	Dutch	gift of God
Janu	Latin	first month
Janus	Latin	of the archway
Japhet	Hebrew	may he expand
Jaques	French	supplanter
Jarah	Hebrew	sweet as honey
Jared	Hebrew	descending
Jariath	Hebrew	tributary lord
Jarom	Greek	he will rise up
Jaron	Hebrew	he will sing
Jarrett	English	strong with a spear
Jaser	Arabic	fearless
Jason	Hebrew	God is my salvation
Jaspal	Hindi	pure, chaste

Jasper	Persian	he holds treasure
Jatan	Hindi	saintly man
Javan	Hebrew	Greek man
Javas	Hindi	keen-eyed
Jay	Sanskrit	victorious
Jaydon	Hebrew	he will judge
Jaymin	Hebrew	son of the right hand
Jeb	Hebrew	friend of God
Jebediah	Hebrew	friend of God
Jed	Hebrew	friend of God
Jedi	Hebrew	God knows, protects
Jehiel	Hebrew	may God live
Jehoash	Hebrew	YAHWEH has given
Jehoichin	Hebrew	God will fortify
Jehoram	Hebrew	exalted by YAHWEH
Jehoshaphat	Hebrew	the Lord judges
Jehu	Hebrew	he is God
Jehudi	Hebrew	of the tribe of Judah
Jem	Hebrew	supplanter
Jenda	Hebrew	God is gracious
Jengo	African	ruddy complexion
Jephtha	Hebrew	God will judge
Jerad	Hebrew	to descend
Jerah	Hebrew	lunar month
Jered	Hebrew	to descend
Jeremias	Hebrew	God will set free
Jeremiel	Hebrew	God will exalt
Jeremy	Hebrew	God will raise up
Jeriah	Hebrew	God has seen
Jericho	Arabic	city of the moon
Jerod	Hebrew	descendant
Jeroen	Arabic	a holy man
Jerome	Greek	of the sacred name
Jerrah	Arabic	gives sweetness

Jerram	Hebrew	exalted by the Lord
Jershon	Hebrew	to inherit
Jesiah	Hebrew	God supports, saves
Jess	Hebrew	God exists, sees all
Jesse	Hebrew	gift from God
Jesus	Hebrew	God is my salvation
Jethro	Hebrew	man of abundance
Ji	Asian	organized
Jimmy	English	supplanter
Jin	Asian	treasured, golden
Jing	Asian	flawless
Jiri	African	from the fruitful forest
Jivin	Hindi	giver of life
Joab	Hebrew	to praise God
Joachim	Hebrew	established by God
Joash	Hebrew	God has given
Job	Hebrew	persecuted
Jocheved	Hebrew	the glory of God
Jody	English	God will add
Joed	Hebrew	God is witness
Joel	Hebrew	Jehovah is God
John	Hebrew	God is gracious
Joji	Asian	he who works the earth
Jolon	Nat. Am.	from cold oak tree valley
Jomar	Hebrew	handsome
Jomei	Asian	one who spreads light
Jomo	African	one who works the earth
Jonah	Hebrew	a dove
Jonas	Hebrew	a dove
Jonathan	Hebrew	a gift of God
Jorah	Hebrew	God has reproached
Joram	Hebrew	Jehovah is exalted
Jordan	Hebrew	the down-flowing river
Jore	Dutch	God will uplift

Jorim	Norse	farmer, worker of earth
Joseph	Hebrew	God will add
Joses	Hebrew	God will increase
Josh	Hebrew	Jehovah is salvation
Joshua	Hebrew	God is salvation
Josiah	Hebrew	God will assist
Joss	Hebrew	God will enlarge
Jotham	Hebrew	God is perfect
Jovan	Latin	majestic, supreme
Jubal	Hebrew	a ram
Judah	Hebrew	one who praises God
Judd	Hebrew	one who praises God
Jude	Hebrew	one who praises God
Juha	Hebrew	gift from God
Julian	Greek	youthful
Julius	Greek	child of love
Juma	African	Friday-born
Jun	Asian	obedient one
June	Latin	youthful
Junien	Hebrew	God will uplift
Juniper	Latin	like the evergreen
Jupiter	Latin	the supreme one
Jurre	Hebrew	God will uplift
Jussi	Hebrew	God is gracious
Justin	Latin	Just and upright

Kabaka	African	a king
Kabir	Hindi	spiritual leader
Kabos	Hebrew	a swindler

Kachada	Nat. Am.	white-skinned man
Kaden	Arabic	beloved companion
Kadir	Arabic	capable, competent
Kaelen	Gaelic	mighty warrior
Kafele	Egyptian	a son to die for
Kafi	African	well behaved, quiet
Kaga	Nat. Am.	historian
Kahale	Island	stays close to home
Kai	African	beautiful
Kai	Asian	continual, unceasing
Kai	Basque	harbor pier
Kai	Celtic	dog
Kai	Burmese	unbreakable
Kai	Cantonese	unceasing
Kai	Celtic	keeper of keys
Kai	Egyptian	spirit, breath
Kai	Estonian	pier
Kai	Greek	and, of the earth
Kai	Hawaiian	sea spray
Kai	Hebrew	life, lives
Kai	Hindi	tea
Kai	Hmong	rewarded servant
Kai	Island	of the sea
Kai	Itsekiri	love
Kai	Japanese	a place of resting
Kai	Latin	rejoice, happiness
Kai	Mandarin	victory, open hearted
Kai	Maori	food
Kai	Navajo	willow tree
Kai	Norse	a small chicken
Kai	Persian	king
Kai	Pima	seed
Kai	Welsh	Sir Cai, knight
Kaimi	Island	the seeker

Kain	Hebrew	one who acquires
Kaj	Norse	of the earth
Kajika	Nat. Am.	silent walker
Kalanath	Hindi	full and bright moon
Kalb	Arabic	dog
Kaleb	Hebrew	aggressive dog
Kaletor	Greek	handsome
Kalev	Hebrew	dog, fierce
Kallon	Greek	handsome
Kalyan	Hindi	happy, prosperous
Kana	Island	ropelike
Kanad	Hindi	an ancient
Kanan	Hindi	from the garden
Kangee	Nat. Am.	raven
Kane	Gaelic	little warrior
Kaniel	Hebrew	the lord supports me
Kano	Asian	powerful man
Kanoa	Island	free
Karam	Arabic	generosity
Karan	Greek	pure, chaste
Kardal	Arabic	of a mustard seed
Kare	Norse	a huge man, giant
Kari	Norse	of the wind
Karmel	Hebrew	of the garden, vineyard
Karmon	Gaelic	lord of the manor
Karpos	Greek	fruit
Karsten	Greek	anointed one
Kashi	Hindi	shining one
Kassa	African	compensated
Kato	Latin	man of good judgement
Kavin	Celtic	handsome man
Kayon	African	long-awaited child
Kazin	Greek	creative man
Keane	Gaelic	cunning warrior

Keanu	Island	cool mountain breeze
Keb	African	of the earth
Kebes	Greek	Phoenician island
Kedem	Hebrew	an old soul
Keefe	Gaelic	handsome, beloved
Kegan	Gaelic	small, fiery man
Keelan	Gaelic	slender man
Keinan	Gaelic	of an ancient family
Kefir	Hebrew	a young lion
Keire	Gaelic	dark-featured
Kelby	Gaelic	farm near a spring
Kele	Nat. Am.	sparrow hawk
Kels	Norse	ship's victory island
Keme	Nat. Am.	secretive man
Ken	Asian	strong, healthy man
Kenan	Celtic	little ancient one
Kenaniah	Hebrew	YAHWEH establishes
Kenaz	Hebrew	bright
Kenyan	Gaelic	blond-haired man
Keos	Hebrew	he will enlarge
Kephas	Aramaic	rock
Kermit	Gaelic	free of envy
Kester	Gaelic	follower of Christ
Ketan	Sanskrit	home
Keva	Gaelic	handsome, beloved
Kibbe	Nat. Am.	nightingale
Kieran	Gaelic	dark featured
Killean	Gaelic	small, fierce
Kim	Asian	precious as gold
Kimball	English	one who leads warriors
Kimnor	Jaredite	father of Akish
Kimon	Greek	dull, sleepy
King	English	royal ruler
Kintan	Hindi	crowned ruler

Kinza	Arabic	treasure of gratitude
Kirin	Hindi	a ray of pure light
Kirphis	Greek	mountain cave
Kirtan	Sanskrit	to repeat, chant, sing
Kirti	Sanskrit	fame, glory
Kish	Hebrew	bow, archer
Kishkumen	Nephite	Gadianton robber
Kitchi	Nat. Am.	brave young man
Kittos	African	precious jewels
Kleopas	Norse	glory, light to father
Klopas	Greek	glorious countenance
Knoton	Nat. Am.	of the wind
Koa	Island	fearless man
Kobe	Hebrew	supplanter
Kohana	Nat. Am.	swift
Konon	Greek	compiler
Korax	Greek	agitator
Korben	Latin	raven-haired man
Koren	Hebrew	gleaming, bright
Koresh	Hebrew	to dig the earth
Korihor	Nephite	a disbeliever, antichrist
Kosmo	Greek	universal man
Kosumi	Nat. Am.	spearer of fish
Kotori	Nat. Am.	screech-owl spirit
Kozma	Greek	decorated man
Kraig	Gaelic	solid as a rock
Krantor	Greek	philosopher
Kreon	Greek	master, ruler
Kreskes	Greek	to grow
Kumen	Nephite	leader
Kumenonhi	Nephite	apostle, leader
Kumi	African	forceful, direct
Kuper	Hebrew	like copper
Kuron	African	one who gives thanks

Kuruk	Nat. Am.	a bear
Kwahu	Nat. Am.	like an eagle
Kwan	Asian	bold character
Kwatoko	Nat. Am.	large-beaked bird
Kye	Island	rejoice
Kyle	Gaelic	from a narrow channel
Kylor	Norse	archer, bowman
Kyran	Arabic	royal, a lord
Kyros	Greek	leader, master

Laban	Hebrew	light hair, light complexion
Labib	Arabic	sensible
Lachlam	Gaelic	from the lake lands
Lachoneus	Greek	a trader
Ladan	Hebrew	alert, aware
Lael	Hebrew	belonging to God
Lagan	Hindi	prompt, ready
Lagos	Greek	meaning unknown
Laith	Arabic	looks like a lion
Lalam	Hindi	best, preferred
Lalo	Latin	he sings lullabies
Laman	Arabic	bright, happy man
Lamech	Hebrew	servant of God, strong
Lameh	Arabic	shining man
Lamoni	Nephite	of Laman, a Lamanite
Lamont	Norse	man of the law, to lay down
Lamus	Latin	from Greek myth
Langundo	Nat. Am.	peaceful man
Lansa	Nat. Am.	man of the spear

Lap	Asian	independent man
Lapidos	Hebrew	carries a torch
Lapu	Nat. Am.	cedar tree bark
Larch	Latin	evergreen tree
Larkin	Gaelic	aggressive
Lavesh	Hindi	a calm man
Lav	Hindi	son of the ram
Lavan	Hebrew	white
Lavi	Hebrew	as one, united
Lazar	Hebrew	helped by God
Le	Asian	filled with joy
Leb	Hebrew	heart
Lehi	Hebrew	jawbone
Lehonti	Nephite	a Lamanite officer
Liebel	Hebrew	lionlike
Leith	Gaelic	from the broad river
Lemuel	Hebrew	belonging to God
Len	Nat. Am.	flute player
Lenno	Nat. Am.	brave man
Leo	Latin	lion
Leon	Greek	lion
Leonidas	Latin	having great strength
Leslie	Gaelic	gray fortress, holly garden
Lethos	Greek	lethargy of lotus flower
Lev	Hebrew	of the heart
Levi	Hebrew	united as one
Leyati	Nat. Am.	a smooth and round head
Li	Asian	great strength
Liam	Gaelic	determined protector
Lian	Asian	of the willow
Lib	Latin	freedom
Lidon	Hebrew	judgment is the Lord's
Lif	Norse	lively, energetic
Limhah	Nephite	commander

Limher	Nephite	soldier
Limhi	Nephite	righteous king
Linus	Greek	blond hair
Lirit	Hebrew	musical
Liron	Hebrew	my song
Lise	Nat. Am.	jumping salmon
Loba	African	one who speaks a lot
Lochan	Hindi	eyes, looking
Logan	Gaelic	from a small hollow
Loki	Norse	trickster
Lokni	Island	handsome red rose
Lonan	Nat. Am.	like a cloud
Lonato	Nat. Am.	flint stone
Lot	Hebrew	veiled, hidden
Loukas	Greek	honor of St. Luke
Loxias	Greek	crooked
Lucas	Latin	surrounded by light
Lucian	Latin	surrounded by light
Ludwig	German	famous warrior
Lukos	Greek	wolf
Lycus	Greek	friend
Lydus	Greek	royalty
Lysias	Greek	destroyer

Mac	Gaelic	son of
Macartan	Gaelic	son of Artan
Macallum	Gaelic	son of Callum
Machau	Hebrew	gift of God
Machum	Hebrew	comfort

Madan	Hindi	god of love
Mads	Hebrew	gift of God
Maeon	Greek	mythological prophet
Magail	Eblaite	who is like God
Magal	Hebrew	reaper, harvester
Magne	Latin	a great man
Mahad	Sanskrit	great
Mahah	Hebrew	to linger, tarry
Mahalah	Hebrew	dance, harp, tender
Mahali	Hebrew	weary
Mahi	Hindi	farmer
Mahir	Arabic	skilled one
Mahkah	Nat. Am.	of the earth
Maichail	Hebrew	gift from God
Makis	Hebrew	gift from God
Makya	Nat. Am.	eagle hunter, chase lover
Mal	Hindi	gardener
Mal	Hebrew	God's messenger
Malachi	Hebrew	messenger of God
Malak	Arabic	angel
Malki	Hebrew	my king
Mallow	Gaelic	of the river Allo
Malo	Island	victorious man
Mamo	African	small boy
Manaem	Greek	comforter
Manahem	Latin	king of Israel
Manan	Sanskrit	ponder, reflection
Manas	Hindi	spiritual intention
Manasseh	Hebrew	forgetful
Mandar	Hindi	fruit of a sacred tree
Mani	African	from the mountain
Manik	Sanskrit	pink to deep red gem
Mannan	Arabic	benevolent
Manti	Egyptian	a prince, a place name

Manuel	Spanish	Emmanuel, God with us
Marcus	Latin	dedicated to Mars
Mark	Latin	god of war, planet
Marlas	Greek	from the high tower
Marnin	Hebrew	one who brings joy
Maro	Asian	myself
Marom	Hebrew	from the peak
Maron	Hebrew	a flock of sheep
Mars	Latin	the planet Mars, war god
Marwan	Arabic	generous, solid stone
Masa	African	centered
Maska	Nat. Am.	great strength
Masos	Hebrew	filled with happiness
Matai	Hebrew	gift of God
Mathe	Celtic	a bear
Mathoni	Hebrew	gift, second-born twin
Mathonihah	Hebrew	gift, first-born twin
Matoskah	Nat. Am.	white bear
Matthew	Hebrew	gift of YAHWEH
Maximilian	Latin	topmost, greatest
Mayir	Latin	large man
Medad	Hebrew	beloved friend
Medon	Greek	loudly proclaim, sound
Medus	Greek	driven to rule, king
Meer	Arabic	leader, ruler
Meged	Hebrew	blessed with goodness
Meges	Greek	led forty ships
Meir	Hebrew	he who illuminates
Mekina	Hopi	warm up
Mel	Gaelic	millworker
Meli	Nat. Am.	one who is bitter
Melas	Greek	black flower, eight myths
Melchior	Arabic	king, city
Melchisedek	Hebrew	my God is righteousness

Mele	Island	one who is happy
Melech	Semitic	king
Memnon	Greek	warrior king
Menachem	Hebrew	he provides comfort
Menassah	Hebrew	causing to forget
Mendel	German	one who comforts
Mendon	Nat. Am.	water, fish
Menefer	Egyptian	of the beautiful city
Mentor	Greek	wise guide, way-shower
Merari	Egyptian	beloved, strong
Mercury	Latin	messenger of commerce
Meshach	Hebrew	enduring, strong
Meshullam	Hebrew	man sent on a mission
Methuselah	Hebrew	his death shall bring water
Meton	Greek	from the astronomer, engineer
Metron	Greek	an inexact measurement
Meyer	Hebrew	he who illuminates
Miach	Gaelic	medic, healer
Michael	Hebrew	he who is like God
Michio	Asian	strength of thousands
Midas	Greek	a golden touch
Migdal	Hebrew	from the tower
Miki	Asian	from the trees
Milan	Sanskrit	happy gathering
Milan	Latin	hardworking man
Milap	Nat. Am.	charitable man
Miner	Latin	works the mines
Mingan	Nat. Am.	the gray wolf
Minos	Greek	labyrinth-maker
Mirit	Hebrew	a bitter man
Miron	Greek	fragrant plant, myrrh
Mirsab	Arabic	judicious
Misi	Hebrew	gift of God
Miska	Hebrew	like God

Misu	Nat. Am.	troubled, rippling brook
Mitchell	English	who is like God?
Misu	Nat. Am.	from the rippling water
Moab	Hebrew	plateau
Mochni	Nat. Am.	talking bird
Moeshe	Hebrew	drawn from water
Mohak	Oriya	an attractive man
Mohammed	Arabic	greatly praised, prophet
Mohan	Hindi	enchanting, delightful
Mojag	Nat. Am.	never quiet, noisy one
Moki	Nat. Am.	mule deer
Moloni	Mayan	volcano water
Mordecai	Hebrew	little man
Morianton	Egyptian	beloved of Aten
Mormon	Egyptian	a place name
Moroni	Arabic	heart of fire
Moronihah	Arabic/Mayan	fire quenched by water
Morven	Celtic	from the mountain gap
Moses	Egyptian	saved from the water
Mosheh	Hebrew	savior
Mosi	Bantu	smoke
Mosiah	Hebrew	advocate, strive for justice
Moti	Hebrew	little man
Mottel	Hebrew	warrior
Moyo	African	of the heart
Muir	Celtic	of the moor
Mulek	Hebrew	little king
Muloki	Eblaite	little king to rule
Munir	Arabic	luminous man
Murad	Arabic	wish, desire
Murel	Gaelic	of the shining sea
Murli	Hindi	flute
Murow	Celtic	sea warrior
Musa	Arabic	a savior

Musad	Arabic	lucky man
Muti	Arabic	obedient one
Mydon	Greek	Trojan soldier myth
Myron	Greek	fragrant myrrh oil

Naal	Gaelic	celebrated saint
Naaman	Hebrew	pleasant man
Naaz	Hindi	proud man
Nabil	Arabic	highborn man
Naboo	Babylonian	wisdom, writing god myth
Nachman	Hebrew	comforter of others
Nada	Arabic	coated by morning dew
Nadab	Hebrew	liberal man
Nadav	Hebrew	generous man
Nadim	Arabic	beloved friend
Nadish	Hindi	of the sea
Nadiv	Hebrew	noble one
Nadeen	Arabic	hopeful man
Nadeem	Arabic	friend, companion
Nadish	Hindi	sea, cannot be harmed
Nadiv	Hebrew	noble one
Naftali	Hebrew	struggling man
Nagid	Hebrew	great ruler, leader
Nahele	Island	forest, woods
Nahele	Nat. Am.	man of the forest
Nahor	Hebrew	bright, clearheaded
Nahum	Arabic	grieve, complain
Nahum	Hebrew	compassionate man
Naim	Arabic	content man

Z

Naji	Arabic	safe, protected
Nalin	Hindi	lotus flower
Naman	Hindi	friendly man
Nandan	Hindi	pleasing
Nanten	Nat. Am.	a spokesman, speaker
Naoum	Hebrew	one who comforts
Narcissus	Greek	self-loving man
Naren	Hindi	best among all men
Naresh	Hindi	a king
Nassar	Arabic	triumphant
Nastas	Nat. Am.	curved as foxtail grass
Nastes	Greek	resurrection
Nathaniel	Hebrew	gift of God
Naveed	Arabic	our best wishes
Naveen	Gaelic	handsome, pleasant
Navid	Arabic	judgement, reward
Navon	Hebrew	a wise man
Nawat	Nat. Am.	left-handed man
Nawkaw	Nat. Am.	from the woods
Nay	Arabic	His grace
Nayan	Hindi	eye
Nayati	Nat. Am.	he who wrestles
Nechemya	Hebrew	consoled by God
Neel	Celtic	champion
Neelam	Hindi	blue sapphire
Nehemiah	Hebrew	comforted by YAHWEH
Nehor	Hebrew	illuminated
Neka	Nat. Am.	wild goose
Nekoda	Hebrew	marked
Neleos	Greek	light one, bright
Nemo	Latin	a nobody
Nen	Arabic	from ancient waters
Neo	Greek	new
Nepi	Egyptian	grain god

Nephi	Nephite	cloud
Nephihah	Nephite	cloud water, rain
Nephos	Greek	cloud
Ner	Hebrew	born during Chanukah
Nereus	Greek	water
Neriah	Hebrew	burning light of God
Nero	Latin	powerful, unyielding
Nestor	Greek	traveler, homecoming
Netanyahu	Hebrew	gift of God
Nethaniah	Hebrew	gift of God
Neum	Hebrew	unknown prophet
Nevin	Latin	sacred one, little bone
Nezer	Hebrew	crowned
Nial	Celtic	the champion
Nibal	Arabic	an arrow smith
Nibaw	Nat. Am.	he stands tall
Nicholas	Greek	a victorious people
Nicodemus	Greek	victory of the people
Nicon	Latin	conquest, victory
Nigan	Nat. Am.	surpasses others
Nike	Greek	he brings victory
Nikiti	Nat. Am.	smooth, round head
Nikodemos	Greek	victory of the people
Nilay	Hindi	heaven, habitat
Nilus	Greek	victorious
Nimrah	Arabic	pure, strong
Nimrod	Hebrew	mighty hunter
Nirad	Hindi	of the clouds
Nimrah	Arabic	leopard, fierce
Nirvan	Sanskrit	blowing out, bliss
Nissan	Hebrew	miracle child
Nissim	Hebrew	believer, wondrous boy
Nitis	Nat. Am.	beloved friend
Niyol	Nat. Am.	of the wind

Noach	Hebrew	provides comfort
Noah	Hebrew	peaceful wanderer
Noam	Hebrew	beloved friend
Noble	Latin	wellborn man
Nodin	Nat. Am.	of the wind
Noe	Hebrew	peaceful
Nogah	Hebrew	bright, clear
Nolan	Celtic	noble champion
Noor	Arabic	surrounded by light
Nordin	Norse	handsome
Nosh	Nat. Am.	father, fatherly man
Nova	Latin	new, star-birth energy
Now	Arabic	born of light, energy
Numa	Arabic	pleasant, easygoing
Nuri	Arabic	surrounded by light

Oba	African	leader, king, chief
Obediah	Hebrew	servant of God
Oceane	Greek	of the ocean
Ochi	African	laughing boy
Ochos	Greek	delicate, eggshell
Ode	Egyptian	walking traveler
Ode	Greek	lyric poems
Oded	Hebrew	encouraging, supportive
Odel	Greek	sweet melody, song
Odin	Norse	supreme God of myth
Odysseus	Greek	traveler who roams
Ofer	Hebrew	young deer
Ofir	Hebrew	golden son

Ogin	Asian	undaunted
Ohad	Hebrew	dearly loved
Ohin	African	chief, king, leader
Ohio	Nat. Am.	of the good river
Oji	African	gift-bringer
Oki	Asian	from the ocean's center
Olaf	Norse	last of the ancestors
Oma	Arabic	a commanding man
Omar	Arabic	well spoken, flourishing
Omari	African	from God the highest
Omeet	Hebrew	my light shines
Omega	Hebrew	last great one
Omer	Hebrew	flourishing
Omet	Hebrew	my light
Omner	Nephite	unknown meaning
Omni	Nephite	unknown meaning
Omri	Hebrew	grain, Lord is my light
On	Asian	peaceful man
Onesimus	Greek	useful
Onesiphorus	Greek	bringing profit
Onkar	Hindi	the most pure
Ophir	Arabic	abundance
Ophrah	Hebrew	young deer
Or	Hebrew	surrounded by light
Oracle	Greek	diviner, seer
Oran	Aramaic	surrounded by light
Orane	Greek	flourishing man
Orcus	Latin	mythical underworld
Orel	Latin	the golden one
Ori	Hebrew	light of truth surrounds
Orihah	Jaredite	son of Kib, brightness
Orin	Hebrew	from the pine tree
Orion	Greek	a great hunter
Oris	Hebrew	of the trees

Orius	Greek	golden light
Ornice	Hebrew	a Cedar tree
Oron	Hebrew	a light spirit
Orpheus	Greek	darkness, beautiful voice
Orris	Latin	inventive, clever
Orson	Latin	a bear
Osaze	Hebrew	favored by God
Osee	Latin	salvation
Oshea	Hebrew	kind spirit, saved
Osher	Hebrew	man of good fortune
Osias	Greek	salvation
Osip	Hebrew	added upon
Othniel	Hebrew	God's lion
Otis	Greek	deeply perceptive
Ouray	Nat. Am.	fine arrow
Ourbanos	Greek	city dweller
Ouri	Hebrew	my light
Ourias	Hebrew	YAHWEH is my light
Ovadiah	Hebrew	servant of YAHWEH
Oved	Hebrew	one who worships God
Ovid	Latin	egg, shepherd
Oz	Hebrew	great strength
Ozazias	Greek	YAHWEH is strong
Ozi	Hebrew	my power
Ozihel	Latin	my power is God
Ozzi	Hebrew	great strength

Pa	Island	busy
Paanchi	Egyptian	living one

Pachua	Nat. Am.	water snake
Pachus	Egyptian	He is praised
Pacumeni	Nephite	chief judge
Pagag	Nephite	unknown meaning
Pagiel	Hebrew	God disposes
Pahana	Nat. Am.	lost white brother
Pahoran	Nephite	unknown meaning
Paine	Latin	country man, peasant
Paki	Egyptian	witness, sees the truth
Pallas	Greek	wisdom, knowledge
Palladin	Greek	filled with wisdom
Pallatin	Nat. Am.	tough warrior
Pallu	Hebrew	distinguished
Palma	Latin	successful
Palmer	Latin	palm tree
Palmys	Greek	bearing a palm branch
Paltel	Hebrew	God delivers me
Palti	Hebrew	deliverance
Pan	Greek	shepherd-god myth
Pananjay	Hindi	cloud-like
Pandu	Hindi	pale-skinned man
Panos	Greek	rock-solid
Pantias	Greek	philosophical man
Panya	African	mouselike, silent
Pammon	Greek	prolific
Panagiotis	Greek	all holy
Pandion	Greek	royal, wise
Panna	Hindi	emerald
Param	Sanskrit	supreme being
Paran	Hebrew	ornamental, embellished
Paras	Hindi	touchstone
Paris	Celtic	craftsmen, workers
Parish	Celtic	an ecclesiastical ward
Parley	English	pear tree

Parsa	Arabic	devout, pure
Parth	Hindi	warrior prince
Pascal	Latin	born during Easter
Pat	Latin	noble patrician
Patamon	Nat. Am.	tempest, storm
Patli	Aztec	medicine man
Patron	Latin	rustic, peasant
Patwin	Nat. Am.	manly man
Paul	Latin	humble man
Pavak	Hindi	bright, purifying fire
Pavan	Hindi	a light breeze
Pax	Latin	peaceful man
Paxton	English	peaceful town
Payatt	Nat. Am.	he is coming
Payod	Hindi	a cloud
Payoj	Hindi	lotus flower
Paytah	Nat. Am.	a fiery man
Pazel	Hebrew	treasured by God
Pelagon	Greek	mythological name
Peleg	Hebrew	division
Peregrine	Latin	wanderer
Percy	Latin	hunter, to penetrate hedge
Perez	Hebrew	to break through
Pericles	Greek	an excess of glory
Perine	Latin	adventurer
Peritas	Greek	outcome, result
Pesach	Hebrew	passover
Peter	Greek	solid as a rock
Phanes	Hindi	revealer
Phelan	Gaelic	wolf
Phelix	Latin	happy, fortunate
Pheres	Greek	defender
Phileas	Greek	honorable man
Philemon	Greek	affectionate, loving man

Philetus	Greek	beloved
Philip	Greek	horse fancier
Philo	Greek	loves and is loved
Phineas	Greek	mythological king
Phoenix	Greek	dark red, immortal bird
Photius	Greek	scholarly man
Piki	Maori	chief, ruler, leader
Pilan	Nat. Am.	supreme element
Pin	Asian	filled with joy
Pinchas	Hebrew	oracle, serpent's mouth
Ping	Asian	peaceful
Pinya	Hebrew	faithful man
Pio	Latin	pious man
Pirro	Greek	fiery, red-haired man
Plato	Greek	broad-shouldered
Pollux	Greek	crowned, royal
Polo	African	alligator
Poni	African	second-born son
Pons	Latin	from the bridge
Pontius	Latin	fifth-born child
Poorna	Hindi	complete
Pope	Greek	father
Porat	Hebrew	productive
Poriel	Hebrew	fruit of God
Poseidon	Greek	god of the waters
Powa	Nat. Am.	prosperous man
Pradeep	Hindi	surrounded by light
Pran	Hindi	giver of life
Prana	Hindi	life force, spirit
Praxis	Greek	practical, practice
Prem	Hindi	love
Preto	Latin	important man
Prina	Hindi	contented man
Prince	Latin	royal son

Prochoros	Greek	leader of the dance
Proctor	Latin	steward, watchman
Prosper	Latin	fortunate man
Protus	Greek	gift of prophecy
Pryor	Latin	monastery director
Puma	Latin	mountain lion, cougar
Pusan	Hindi	sage, wise man
Puran	Hindi	complete
Pylas	Greek	portal, gateway
Pyris	Greek	flame, fire, red

Qadar	Arabic	capable, competent
Qadi	Hindi	judge
Qaiser	Arabic	ruler, king
Qaletaqa	Nat. Am.	guardian of the people
Qamar	Arabic	born under the moon
Qasim	Arabic	generous, charitable
Qais	Arabic	firm
Qiao	Asian	handsome
Qimat	Hindi	greatly valued man
Qing	Asian	deep water, ocean
Qochata	Nat. Am.	pale-skinned man
Quade	Latin	fourth-born child
Quana	Nat. Am.	man who smells pleasant
Quant	Latin	of great value, worth
Qued	Nat. Am.	likes decorated clothing
Quentin	Latin	fifth-born child, colorful
Quillan	Gaelic	a cub, small boy
Quimby	Norse	man from the woman's land

Quinn	Gaelic	intelligent counselor
Quirinus	Latin	spear-wielder
Qunoun	Nat. Am.	tall man
Quok	Asian	patriot, loyal
Quon	Asian	luminous, shining
Qusai	Arabic	far off, distant time

Raanan	Hebrew	young-looking man
Rabbani	Arabic	divine
Rabbi	Hebrew	the master
Raby	Arabic	gentle wind
Rabia	African	born in spring
Rach	African	frog
Rachim	Hebrew	shows mercy
Radamays	Egyptian	hero
Radwan	Arabic	delightful man
Rael	African	innocent lamb
Rafael	Hebrew	God has healed
Rafer	Gaelic	prosperous man
Rafi	Arabic	exalted one
Rafiki	African	gentle friend
Rahym	Arabic	compassionate
Rai	Asian	trustworthy
Raidon	Asian	god of thunderstorms
Raimy	African	compassionate man
Rajab	African	glorified man
Rajan	Hindi	king
Raka	Hindi	born on a full moon
Rakesh	Hindi	a king

R

Rakin	Arabic	respectful young man
Ram	Sanskrit	pleasing man, pleasant
Raman	Sanskrit	to make merry
Ramel	Hindi	a godly man, pious
Rami	Arabic	a loving man
Ramses	Egyptian	born of the sun god
Rana	Arabic	"behold, a son!"
Ranen	Hebrew	filled with joy
Ranit	Hebrew	to raise voice in song
Ranon	Hebrew	joyful
Raphael	Hebrew	healed by God
Ras	Latin	to love
Rashad	Arabic	has good judgment
Rasmus	Greek	one dearly loved
Ratan	Hindi	jewel
Ravi	Hindi	of the sun
Ravid	Hebrew	seeker, wanderer
Rayhan	Arabic	favored by God
Raza	Arabic	filled with hope
Razie	Aramaic	the Lord is my secret
Reda	Arabic	content, satisfied
Reem	Hebrew	horned animal
Regan	Gaelic	little ruler
Regent	Latin	born into royalty
Reginald	Latin	king's advisor
Regis	Latin	kingly man, regal
Reilly	Gaelic	outgoing man
Remus	Latin	swift
Reth	African	king
Reuben	Hebrew	behold, a son!
Reuel	Hebrew	a friend of God
Revelin	Celtic	from the renowned land
Rhett	Latin	well-spoken man
Rhodes	Greek	where roses grow

Rigel	Arabic	wanderer, hiker
Rin	Asian	good companion
Riplakish	Jaredite	a hill
Riordan	Gaelic	royal poet, minstrel
Riyad	Arabic	gardens
Rizon	Greek	tree root
Roald	Norse	ruler
Roark	Gaelic	champion
Rogan	Gaelic	red-haired man
Rohan	Sanskrit	one who ascends
Roman	Latin	citizen of Rome
Romney	Gaelic	river, source
Ronald	Norse	king's advisor
Ronan	Gaelic	small swimming seal
Roni	Hebrew	my song
Roshan	Arabic	bright and shining light
Rouvin	Hebrew	behold, a son!
Rowan	Gaelic	red berries, redhead
Rowtag	Nat. Am.	born of fire
Roy	Gaelic	red-haired man
Rozen	Hebrew	great ruler
Rudo	African	loving man
Rudolf	Celtic	spirit of the wolf
Rufus	Latin	red-haired man
Rulon	Nat. Am.	spirited man
Rune	Norse	untold, secret
Ruvim	Hebrew	meaningful one
Ryan	Gaelic	little king, small ruler
Ryu	Asian	a dragon
Ryunen	Asian	willow tree

Saad	Aramaic	the Lord's helper
Saarick	Hindi	small songbird
Sabin	Latin	ancient tribe
Sachary	Gaelic	the Lord remembers
Sachet	Hindi	knowledge of the truth
Sachiel	Hebrew	an archangel
Sadar	Hindi	nobleman, leader
Saffar	Arabic	devout man
Sagar	Hindi	a wise king
Sahen	Arabic	alert, aware
Sakeri	Hebrew	the Lord remembers
Salam	Arabic	provides security
Salamon	Hebrew	peaceful
Salar	Arabic	leader
Salus	Greek	strong, healthy
Salathiel	Hebrew	I have asked of God
Samar	Arabic	darkness of night
Sami	Arabic	gifted, exalted
Samson	Hebrew	bright as the sun
Samuel	Hebrew	his name is God
Sancho	Latin	saintly, holy
Sani	Arabic	brilliant, saintly
Sani	Nat. Am.	old one, wisdom
Santan	Latin	saintly, saintlike
Saoul	Hebrew	asked of God
Sarat	Hindi	a wise man
Sarin	Hindi	helpful
Sasson	Hebrew	joy, pleasure
Sasta	Hindi	one who rules

S

Satya	Hindi	truth
Saul	Hebrew	prayed for
Sean	Gaelic	God is gracious
Seantum	Nephite	chief judge
Seiki	Asian	new star, beginning
Sem	Hebrew	a name
Seraiah	Hebrew	prince of the Lord
Seraphim	Greek	burning angels
Servas	Latin	redeemed
Set	Hebrew	compensated
Seth	Hebrew	appointed
Seva	Greek	not wanting
Sevak	Sanskrit	servant of God
Severin	Latin	strict guidance
Shad	Arabic	commanded, led
Shadrach	Hebrew	led by the moon god
Shamgar	Hebrew	sword
Shane	English	God is gracious
Shantan	Sanskrit	auspicious form
Sharad	Arabic	autumn
Sharan	Hindi	surrender
Sharar	Hebrew	sunrise, dawn
Sharat	Hindi	a season
Shaul	Hebrew	prayed for
Shaunak	Hindi	respected, wise
Shay	Gaelic	admirable man
Shayden	Gaelic	admirable son
Shealtiel	Hebrew	asked of God
Sheel	Hindi	strong ethics
Shel	Hebrew	our son
Shelomo	Hebrew	peace
Shem	Hebrew	well-known name
Shemaiah	Aramaic	heard of Jehovah
Shemer	Hebrew	guard, watchman

Shemnon	Nephite	a disciple, guard
Shemuel	Hebrew	his name is God
Sherem	Unknown	learned, scholarly
Shet	Hebrew	appointed
Shez	Jaredite	king, son
Shiblom	Nephite	commander
Shiblon	Nephite	missionary, historian
Shields	Gaelic	faithful protector
Shilah	Nat. Am.	brotherly
Shilo	Nat. Am.	brother
Shiloh	Hebrew	peaceful, he was sent
Shimon	Hebrew	to hear
Shimshon	Hebrew	bright sun
Shino	Asian	bamboo stem
Shiriki	Nat. Am.	coyote
Shiz	Jaredite	military leader
Shlomo	Hebrew	peace of God
Shubha	Hindi	auspicious, favored
Shule	Germanic	synagogue, school
Si	Asian	gentleman
Sigismund	Germanic	protector of victory
Sigurd	Norse	victorious protector
Sike	Nat. Am.	he sits at home
Silas	Latin	woodland dweller
Simcha	Hebrew	gladness, joy, celebration
Simon	Hebrew	God has heard
Sinai	Hebrew	from the clay desert
Sinon	Hebrew	listening
Sivan	Hebrew	the ninth month
Skah	Nat. Am.	white
Slavin	Gaelic	man of the mountains
Slone	Gaelic	high-ranking warrior
So	Asian	intelligent man
Socrates	Greek	philosopher

Socus	Greek	bright
Sofian	Arabic	devoted man
Sofus	Greek	great wisdom
Sohan	Hindi	handsome man
Sohrab	Arabic	bright, shining
Soko	African	happiness
Sol	Hebrew	peace
Solaris	Greek	of the sun
Solomon	Hebrew	peaceful man
Songaa	Nat. Am.	great strength
Soren	Norse	strict, stern
Spark	Latin	to scatter light
Spencer	English	dispenser of provisions
Stamos	Greek	reasonable man
Stavros	Greek	crowned, royal
Steinar	Norse	rock-solid warrior
Stentor	Greek	powerful voice
Stephen	Greek	crowned with a garland
Stian	Norse	voyager, swift
Strabo	Greek	historian, philosopher
Straton	Greek	army, warriors
Sudi	African	successful man
Sujay	Hindi	a good victory
Sukarno	African	the chosen one
Sukumar	Hindi	a tender man
Sukant	Hindi	charming man
Sule	African	adventurous man
Sullivan	Gaelic	dark-eyed
Sultan	African	ruler
Suman	Hindi	wise man
Sunder	Hindi	lovely man
Sur	Hindi	a melody, intelligent
Suram	Hindi	beautiful
Suran	Hindi	pleasant sound

Sutara	Hindi	holy star, bright
Sven	Norse	a lad, youthful
Svyatoslav	Slavic	brightness, glory
Sweeney	Gaelic	brave young hero
Sylvester	Latin	man from the forest
Symetris	African	fortunate man
Syon	Hindi	followed by good fortune

Taaveti	Hebrew	dearly loved
Tab	Latin	brilliant
Taban	Gaelic	genius
Tabor	Hebrew	difficult, struggle
Tacary	African	strong as a warrior
Tacitus	Latin	historian
Tadi	Nat. Am.	of the wind
Taggart	Gaelic	son of a priest
Taghee	Nat. Am.	a chief
Taha	Island	firstborn child
Tahir	Arabic	pure, chaste, clean
Tahoe	Nat. Am.	from the big water
Tahoma	Nat. Am.	snowy mountain peak
Tai	Asian	talented one
Taima	Nat. Am.	of the thunder
Taine	Gaelic	of the river
Takoda	Nat. Am.	a friend to all
Tal	Hebrew	covered in morning dew
Talib	Arabic	seeker of knowledge
Talmai	Aramaic	hill, mound, furrow
Talos	Greek	giant, island protector

Tam	Asian	having a caring heart
Tam	Hebrew	one who is truthful
Taman	Hindi	one who is needed
Tamar	Hebrew	from the palm tree
Tamir	Arabic	wealthy man
Tamir	Hebrew	a tall man, honored
Tamas	Aramaic	a twin
Tan	Asian	a high achiever
Tanak	Hindi	reward
Tanay	Hindi	beloved son
Taneli	Hebrew	will be judged of God
Tanish	Hindi	ambitious man
Tanmay	Hindi	absorbed, dedicated
Tanner	English	maker of leather
Tano	African	of the river
Tansy	Greek	immortal
Tansy	Nat. Am.	like a flower
Tanul	Sanskrit	expansive
Tanveer	Hindi	brave, strong
Tarak	Hindi	protecter of others
Taral	Hindi	honeybee
Taran	Gaelic	of the thunder
Taranga	Hindi	of the waves
Tarchon	Etruscan	originator, founder
Tarmon	Gaelic	of the church's land
Tarn	Norse	from the mountain pool
Taro	Asian	a big boy, firstborn son
Tarquin	Latin	impulsive, a king
Taru	Hindi	good swimmer
Tarun	Hindi	youthful man
Tatanka	Nat. Am.	prairie buffalo
Tate	English	brings happiness
Tavish	Celtic	from the hillside
Tay	Gaelic	from the river

Taylor	English	clothing maker
Teancum	Mayan	unknown hieroglyphs
Teancum	Nephite	great military leader
Tecton	Greek	designer, engineer
Teetonka	Nat. Am.	big talker, big lodge
Teiko	Norse	centered, hits mark
Teirnon	Celtic	a regal man
Tekoa	Hebrew	notes of the trumpet
Telamon	Greek	mythological hunter
Tellis	Greek	wisdom, a wise man
Teman	Hebrew	of the right hand
Tendo	Greek	heel, tendon
Tenen	African	born on a Monday
Teomner	Mayan	unknown hieroglyphs
Teomner	Nephite	military officer
Teppo	Norse	a crown, weapon
Terah	Hebrew	a wild goat
Terran	Celtic	man of the earth
Tertius	Greek	third-born child
Tesher	Hebrew	gift of God
Teshi	African	filled with laughter
Tessema	African	people listen to him
Tet	Asian	New Year's baby
Tevah	Hebrew	a natural man
Tevel	Hebrew	dearly loved
Thabo	African	filled with happiness
Thaddeus	Aramaic	having heart
Than	Asian	a brilliant man
Theodore	Greek	gift from God
Theophilus	Greek	loved by God
Theos	Greek	God
Theron	Greek	a great hunter
Tho	Asian	having a long life
Thomas	Aramaic	one of twins

Thor	Norse	god of thunder
Thorald	Norse	follower of Thor
Thorbert	Norse	shines with Thor's glory
Thorbjorn	Norse	Thor's bear
Thorolf	Norse	Thor's wolf
Thurl	Celtic	from the strong fortress
Tiernan	Gaelic	lord of the manor
Tiis	Nat. Am.	of the cottonwoods
Tilak	Hindi	a great leader
Tillman	Gaelic	he plows the earth
Tilon	Hebrew	a generous man
Tilton	Gaelic	a fertile estate
Timon	Greek	a respected man
Timothy	Greek	one who honors God
Tin	Asian	a great thinker
Tipu	Hindi	tiger
Tiras	Hebrew	desirable
Tirta	Asian	water
Tisa	African	ninth-born
Titir	Hindi	partridge
Titos	Greek	go to honor
Titus	Latin	honorable
Toan	Asian	one who is safe
Tobiah	Hebrew	YAHWEH is good
Tobias	Greek	God is good
Tobin	Gaelic	God is good
Tocho	Nat. Am.	mountain lion
Tokala	Nat. Am.	dark fox
Tovi	Hebrew	the Lord is good
Toyo	Asian	man of plenty
Tracy	Gaelic	tall, warlike
Triston	Celtic	a knight, sad
Tsin	Nat. Am.	horse rider
Tu	Asian	quick-minded

Tuari	Nat. Am.	a young eagle
Tubaloth	Nephite	Lamanite king
Tufan	Hindi	storm, tempest
Tuhin	Hindi	from the snow
Tuka	Hindi	young boy
Tukaram	Hindi	holy poet
Tuketu	Nat. Am.	bear stirs dust
Tulsidaas	Hindi	devoted man
Tulsikumar	Hindi	son of a holy man
Tunava	Hindi	tune from a flute
Tunda	Norse	a treeless plain
Tungar	Sanskrit	high, lofty
Tungesh	Nat. Am.	boy
Tungish	Hindi	Lord Shiva, Lord Vishnu
Tupi	Nat. Am.	to pull up
Turbo	Latin	spinning, spiral
Turag	Hindi	a thought, idea
Tusita	Asian	heaven-sent
Tut	Egyptian	courageous man
Tutyahu	Hebrew	goodness of God
Tuvya	Hebrew	God is good
Tybalt	Latin	truth-seeker
Tychon	Greek	accurate
Tydeus	Greek	father
Tyee	Nat. Am.	great chieftain
Tynan	Gaelic	dark, dusty
Tyr	Norse	ancient god
Tyris	Latin	from ancient Tyre
Tyron	Gaelic	from Owen's land
Tzadok	Hebrew	just, fair
Tzion	Hebrew	from the mountain
Tziyon	Hebrew	son of Zion
Tzivah	Hebrew	hosts
Tzuriel	Hebrew	God is my strength

Tzvi	Hebrew	a deer

U

U	Asian	gentle, kind man
Uba	African	lord of the house
Udar	Hindi	generous man
Udayan	Hindi	thriving
Udeh	Hebrew	praising God
Udi	Hebrew	torch-carrier
Udo	African	prosperous
Ukiah	Nat. Am.	from the deep valley
Ulick	Gaelic	young William
Ull	Norse	glory, justice
Ultan	Gaelic	from the north
Ulysses	Latin	roaming traveller
Umar	Arabic	prosperous
Umi	African	giver of life
Unni	Norse	modest
Uni	Latin	united as one
Urban	Latin	city dweller
Urbanus	Norse	courteous
Uri	Hebrew	the Lord is my light
Urias	Celtic	light of the Lord
Uriel	Hebrew	the angel of light
Ursus	Latin	a bear
Usher	Latin	mouth of the river
Utt	Arabic	kind, wise
Uzzi	Hebrew	having great power
Uzziah	Hebrew	the Lord is my strength
Uzziel	Hebrew	God is mighty

Vada	Hebrew	like a rose
Vadin	Hindi	a speaker
Vairat	Hindi	a gemstone
Valentine	Latin	strong, healthy
Vali	Norse	son of myth
Valin	Hindi	monkey king
Van	Asian	of the clouds
Vandan	Hindi	salutation
Vanir	Norse	of the ancient gods
Varid	Hindi	descending
Varin	Hebrew	superior
Varius	Latin	versatile
Varney	Celtic	alder tree grove
Varune	Hindi	lord of the waters
Vaschel	Hebrew	a small ash tree
Vasu	Hindi	kind, bright
Ve	Norse	brother of myth
Ved	Sanskrit	great knowledge
Velvel	Hebrew	a wolf
Victor	Latin	champion
Vidar	Norse	forest warrior
Viho	Nat. Am.	chief, leader
Vijay	Hindi	conquerer
Vikas	Hindi	one who progresses
Viking	Norse	a seafarer
Vincent	Latin	a conquerer
Vir	Hindi	brave, traveller
Virgil	Latin	staff-bearer
Vito	Latin	one who gives life

V

Vivek	Hindi	filled with wisdom
Von	Norse	filled with hope
Vulcan	Latin	god of fire

Waban	Nat. Am.	east wind
Wafi	Arabic	trustworthy
Wahkan	Nat. Am.	sacred one
Wail	Arabic	seeking shelter
Wapi	Nat. Am.	fortunate
Wara	Aboriginal	man of the water
Warun	Aboriginal	of the sky
Wasay	Arabic	boundless, no limit
Wei	Asian	brilliant, strong
Wematin	Nat. Am.	brotherly
Wicasa	Nat. Am.	wise one
Wilford	English	from the willow ford
Wilfred	English	wishes for peace
Winton	English	from the pastureland
Wu	Asian	an alchemist
Wuyi	Nat. Am.	soaring turkey vulture
Wynono	Nat. Am.	firstborn child

WX

| Xan | Hebrew | well fed |
| Xander | Greek | defender of mankind |

Xanthos	Greek	blond-haired man
Xavier	Arabic	bright, intelligent
Xwnon	Greek	stranger in the land
Ximon	Hebrew	God has heard
Xi	Asian	happiness
Xue	Asian	studious man
Xun	Asian	swift running man
Xuthus	Greek	founder of nations
Xylon	Greek	forest dweller

Yaakov	Hebrew	supplanter
Yabliss	Arabian	of the desert land
Yachin	Hebrew	He will establish
Yadid	Hebrew	dearly loved man
Yadon	Hebrew	the Lord will judge
Yael	Hebrew	fruitful, strength
Yagil	Hebrew	celebrate, rejoice
Yago	Hebrew	supplants
Yahto	Nat. Am.	color blue, blue eyes
Yahya	Arabic	God is gracious
Yair	Hebrew	he will light, enlighten
Yakar	Hebrew	precious son
Yakecan	Nat. Am.	he sings to the sky
Yakov	Hebrew	replace, renew
Yamal	Hindi	one of twins
Yan	Hebrew	God is gracious
Yancy	Hindi	an Englishman
Yanis	Greek	God is gracious
Yanive	Hebrew	prosperous man

Yankel	Hebrew	supplanter, to renew
Yaotle	Aztec	great warrior
Yaphet	Hebrew	handsome
Yar	Latin	year, calendar of days
Yardan	Arabic	down-flowing river
Yared	Hebrew	descent
Yarema	Hebrew	appointed of God
Yarin	Hebrew	understanding
Yaron	Hebrew	to lift a voice in praise
Yas	Nat. Am.	child of the snow
Yash	Hindi	glorious man
Yavin	Hebrew	he will understand
Yasin	Arabic	prosperous man
Yazid	Arabic	striving to improve
Yebadia	Hebrew	a gift from God
Yechezkel	Hebrew	strengthened by God
Yechiel	Hebrew	may God live
Yedidiah	Hebrew	beloved of God
Yeeshai	Hebrew	a valuable gift
Yefet	Hebrew	handsome, great
Yehoash	Hebrew	God's fire
Yehochanan	Hebrew	God is gracious
Yehonatan	Hebrew	God has given
Yehoram	Hebrew	God is praised
Yehoshua	Hebrew	God rescues
Yehu	Hebrew	God is eternal
Yehudi	Hebrew	he who praises God
Yered	Hebrew	renewal
Yerik	Hebrew	appointed by God
Yeshua	Hebrew	salvation
Yigol	Hebrew	shall be redeemed
Yishai	Hebrew	of substance, revered
Yiska	Nat. Am.	night has passed
Yitro	Hebrew	abundance

Yoash	Hebrew	God has strength
Yoav	Hebrew	praise, God is father
Yochanan	Hebrew	God is gracious
Yoel	Hebrew	God is willing
Yogi	Hindi	mystic ascetic
Yohan	Hebrew	God is gracious
Yoram	Hebrew	God is exalted
Yordan	Hebrew	down-flowing river
Yosef	Hebrew	God will add
Yoshi	Asian	free, good-hearted
Yotam	Hebrew	perfection is God
Yu	Asian	born in rain, honored
Yuki	Asian	man of snow, fortunate
Yuma	Nat. Am.	son of a chief
Yusuf	Arabic	added upon, abundant
Yuu	Asian	topmost, admirable
Yuval	Hebrew	a ram

Zabian	Arabic	celestial body adorer
Zabulon	Hebrew	exalted
Zaccharias	Hebrew	the Lord remembers
Zaci	African	god of fatherhood
Zadok	Hebrew	righteous man
Zafar	Arabic	a victorious man
Zale	Greek	strength of the sea
Zaman	Arabic	keeper of time
Zameel	Arabic	beloved friend
Zamir	Hebrew	songbird
Zan	Hebrew	well fed

Zane	English	God is gracious
Zani	Hebrew	gift of God
Zarab	African	guardian, protector
Zarek	Greek	God protect the king
Zarahemla	Hebrew	seed, child of compassion
Zarahemla	Nephite	a people, place name, red sea
Zared	Hebrew	one who has been trapped
Zavad	Hebrew	bestowal, a gift from God
Zaxaria	Hebrew	YAHWEH remembers
Zayit	Hebrew	from the olive tree
Ze	Latin	God will add
Zebadiah	Hebrew	gift from God
Zebedee	Greek	YAHWEH has bestowed
Zebulon	Hebrew	exalted
Zechariah	Hebrew	YAHWEH remembers
Zed	Hebrew	justice
Zedekiah	Hebrew	justice of YAHWEH
Zeezrom	Nephite	solicitor, law of Moses
Zelig	German	one who is blessed
Zelophehad	Hebrew	protection from terror
Zemnarihah	Hebrew	melody, song, singing
Zen	Asian	enlightened
Zenephi	Nephite	commander
Zeniff	Nephite	king, record-keeper
Zenock	Hebrew	prophet of Israel
Zenos	Hebrew	prophet of Israel
Zephan	Hebrew	hidden by God
Zephaniah	Hebrew	YAHWEH remembers
Zerahemnah	Hebrew	seed of compassion
Zeram	Hebrew	stream
Zethus	Greek	of Zeus
Zevadyah	Hebrew	friend of YAHWEH
Zevulun	Hebrew	dwelling of honor
Zia	Arabic	brilliantly glowing man

Ziba	Hebrew	station
Ziff	Hebrew	a wolf
Zimra	Hebrew	my praise, my song
Zimran	Arabic	a song of praise
Zimri	Hebrew	my praise, my song
Zinan	Asian	second-born son
Zindel	Hebrew	defender of mankind
Zion	Hebrew	from the citadel
Ziv	Hebrew	a radiant man
Zo	African	spiritual counselor
Zohar	Hebrew	surrounded by light
Zopyros	Greek	a glowing man
Zoram	Hebrew	YAHWEH is my brother
Zoticus	Greek	full of life
Zubin	Arabic	honored, best
Zuriel	Hebrew	the Lord is my rock

Appendix: References for Further Study and Tips for New Parents

The library at Alexandria in Egypt was organized sometime around 300 BC and was considered the repository of all human knowledge until it was partially destroyed by Julius Caesar, who "accidently" burned it down while firing at ships in the Alexandrian War of 48 BC. The Aurelians attacked in AD 270–275, and Coptic Pope Theophilus decreed it destroyed in AD 391, lest any new thought creep into the minds of the masses who studied there. The Muslim conquest of AD 642 pretty much finished it off, and though rumors persist of a massive earthquake toppling it, nothing is known for certain except that it is no longer there.

For most of us, knowledge is a mouse-click away. Wonderful resources exist to help us find our own family names. A few are included in links below. Once you have selected some choice names for your little one, you may study about the names and the men and women who have borne them through the ages. Some day, your children may want to learn these stories.

Many wonderful websites exist to help you learn more about these names. Tara and Mike Campbell have a well-researched site in Canada called "Behind The Name," which you can find at http://www.behindthename .com/names. Books are available everywhere to aid in further research, from some with over 100,000 names to *The Last Word on First Names* by Linda Rosenkrantz and Pamela Redmond. Though the book is a bit dated (which happens fast in the baby-naming world) the authors carry on fascinating dialogue, like "Hope is hot; Hortense is not" to help you through the minefield of what is acceptable and what no longer works for naming your beloved offspring.

helpful websites

http://en.wikipedia.org/wiki/Onomastics

http://en.wikipedia.org/wiki/List_of_Greek_and_Latin_roots_in_ English

http://www.learnthat.org/pages/view/roots.html

http://wordinfo.info/

http://www.behindthename.com/glossary/view/linguistics

http://www.factmonster.com/ipka/A0907017.html

https://www.familysearch.org/

http://www.ancestry.com

http://www.onegreatfamily.com

http://www.worldvitalrecords.com/

http://www.origins.net/

http://www.genesreunited.co.uk/

http://www.genealogy.com

http://usgenweb.org/

http://www.progenealogists.com/top50genealogy2009.htm

references

John Tvedtnes, *Authentic Ancient Names and Words in the Book of Abraham and Related Kirtland Egyptian Papers,* 2005 FAIR Conference.

Hugh Nibley, *Abraham in Egypt* (Salt Lake City: Deseret Book, 1981), 193–94.

John Lundquist, "Was Abraham in Elba?" in *Studies in Scripture II: The Pearl of Great Price,* ed. Robert L. Millet and Kent Jackson (Salt Lake City: Randall, 1985).

John Gee and Brian M. Hauglid, eds. *Astronomy, Papyrus, and Covenant* (Provo, Utah: Foundation for Ancient Research and Mormon Studies, 2005).

Hugh Nibley, "The Prophetic Book of Mormon," ed. John Welch, vol. 8 in *The Collected Works of Hugh Nibley* (Salt Lake City: Deseret Book and F.A.R.M.S., 1989), 281–82.

Paul Hoskisson, "What's in a Name?" *Journal of Book of Mormon Studies* 7, no. 1 (2005), 72–73.

Joachim Krecher, "Sumerogramme und Syllabische Orthographie in den Texten aus Ebla," *La Lingua di Ebla*, Series Minor XXII, ed. Luigi Cagni, Napoli: Istituto Universitario Orientale, Dipartimento di Studi Asiatici.

Terrence L. Szink, "The Personal Name 'Alma' at Ebla," *Religious Educator,* no. 1, *(*2000), 53–56.

Michael R. Ash, *Of Faith and Reason: Scholarly Evidences Supporting Joseph Smith* (Springville, UT: Cedar Fort, 2008), 191.

Geoffrey William Bromiley, *The International Standard Bible Encyclopedia: Q-Z* (Grand Rapids, MI: Wm. B. Eerdmans Publishing, 1995), 1211.

T.J. Buckton, *Notes and Queries,* (New York: Oxford University Press, 1854), 10.

Sue Browder, *The New Age Baby Name Book* (New York: Workman Publishing, 1998), 393.

Edward Callary, *Place names of Illinois* (Champaign, IL: University of Illinois Press, 2009), 425.

Richard Stephen Charnock, *Prænomina; or, The etymology of the principal Christian names of Great Britain and Ireland* (London: Trübner & Co., Ludgate Hill, 1882), 128.

Ronan Coghlan, *Irish First Names* (Belfast, Ireland: Appletree Press, 1985), 72.

A.M. Grussi, *Chats on Christian Names* (Whitefish, MT: Kessinger Publishing, 2006), 460.

John Lang, *Six Poets from the Mountain South: Southern literary studies* (Baton Rouge, LA: LSU Press, 2010), 209.

Xiaoan Liu, *Best Chinese Names: your guide to auspicious names* (Singapore: Asiapac Books Pte Ltd, 2005), 200.

John Murry, *The Cornhill Magazine* January–June (London: Smith, Elder & Co, XXIII:1871), 760.

Teresa Norman, *A World of Baby Names* (New York: Perigee Trade, 2003), 640.

Fragrance O'Boyle, *Irish Baby Names* (Santa Rosa, CA: IBN Publishing, 2008), 228.

Robert L. Reid, "Alma's Castle and the Symbolization of Reason in the Faerie Queene," *The Journal of English and Germanic Philology* 80, no.4 (October 1981), 80.

Thomas W. Sheehan, *Dictionary of Patron Saints' Names* (Huntington, IN: Our Sunday Visitor Publishing, 2001), 593.

Henry Woldmar Ruoff, *The Standard Dictionary of Facts: history, language, literature, biography, geography, travel, art, government, politics, industry, invention, commerce, science, education, natural history, statistics and miscellany* (Emeryville, CA: The Frontier Press Company, 1909), 908.

M. Sue Bergin, "Families that Flourish," *BYU Magazine* (Spring 2012), 36–41

A Guide for New Parents

MANY COMPLAIN WHEN THEY DON'T GET AN INSTRUCTION MANUAL DELIVERED with a new baby, so I will attempt a short one here as a bonus. As a former nanny to twenty-six children, as a mother of five, and as a grandmother to two, I am at least qualified to share what helped me along the way.

communication

Listen to your baby. Babies have unique ways of letting you know their needs. Get to know them, and they will tell you in their own way.

Talk to your baby. Even a newborn understands. I learned this from Dr. Peter Sol, our pediatrician, when I wasn't getting enough sleep with my first baby. He sat our baby on the end of the examination table and got down to his eye level. He then waited for his undivided attention. He told him, "Mommy needs sleep. When it is dark (he turned out the light), you must be asleep, or be quiet." It worked. As long as I attended to my son's needs first, he let me sleep. Not eight hours of course—no newborn can manage that—but four to six was a terrific improvement. Keeping him in darkness seemed to signal a sleep cycle for him, and he stayed awake longer during the daylight hours. Plus, none of my children were ever afraid of the dark.

If you learn to listen to your baby's needs and communicate your own, you'll both be blessed. Keep it up as your children grow, and you will never experience "terrible twos," difficult adolescents, or defiant teens. Communication solves most everything.

As far as your communication with others goes, it ended when your child took his first breath. No more hour-long phone or Skype sessions. Email and Facebook are for times when your children are asleep. You must be present in your child's life, and if you keep saying, "Shhhh! Mommy's on the cell," he will suffer. Phone calls are good to take at the park or pool, where you and a lifeguard both have eyes on her, and you can continue to engage her with a cheerful nod or thumbs up.

If you must work from home, be certain to take frequent breaks so your children will know they can count on you caring for and about them.

expectations

Learn what to expect at each stage of your child's life. Most doctors offices have free subscriptions to magazines that showcase what a baby should do each week for the fist six weeks and each month thereafter. Learning what is considered normal for each child at any given time can help you gauge what is right for your child. Of course, yours will be brighter and far more advanced than the magazines suggest, but this can help you spot a problem if something isn't quite right. Deafness may not be detected for years unless you know how to find it.

A child under the age of one cannot be spoiled. Attend to their needs, and they have little reason to cry. Remember, babies do not have the experience to do anything on purpose; they only react to what is given to them. Babies do not conspire against you.

Don't expect your child to be able to shoot baskets at age three because you saw a kid do it on YouTube. Enjoy your little person, and give him or her time to become him-or herself. Pushing only frustrates both of you.

When he or she shows an interest in something, support it. Never be responsible for quashing a child's dream. Warning: keep up with him or her. You don't want to sacrifice to buy your daughter a piano, only to find she now wants to collect frogs, and piano was so last week. You can save a lot of hair-pulling by taking your children to the library to learn all about a subject and see if they really want to jump in, or if it was merely a passing fancy.

expenditures

Until a child is old enough to ask for it, no child needs anything new. The money you save buying secondhand toys and clothing can be invested in a college or vacation fund. As they grew, we told our children, "We don't buy anything advertised on TV." Our thinking was, paying for such advertising made the toys cost more than they were worth. It worked wonderfully, and we were able to let the children judge the difference when we took them shopping. Our grandchildren are still playing with the good investments selected by our children. When they discover you did buy something they saw on TV, your answer is, "Yes! It was on sale, so it was worth it this time," or "I didn't see the commercial." Whichever is true. Always tell the truth.

Exceptions: car seats need to be safe and to be safely installed. Shoes must be new. Wearing worn, secondhand shoes can lead to a lifetime of foot problems. Fortunately, tests have concluded that cheaper athletic shoes are just as durable and good for a foot as expensive name-brand shoes, as long as they aren't constructed of all man-made materials, which can make the feet perspire. Babies don't need shoes at all. Remember those hard, white leather high-tops from the 1920s to the 2000s? What were we thinking?

You can save money, half a forest, and lots of landfill space if you use cotton diapers and launder them yourselves or use a diaper service. An added bonus? No diaper rashes. Parents complain that they have to change baby more often, but ask yourself, do you really want to have your child sit in that "disposable" until it explodes? Didn't think so. Natural "wraps" eliminate the need for diaper pins or old-fashioned plastic pants, and they are simple to sew. Knowing when they are wet helps condition a child so when it is time for toilet training, the task is simple.

love

Think of the family you start as a home or a garden. It needs to be built or nourished to grow. If you ever tear it down, you must start all over again. It is much more difficult with relationships, as, once torn, trust is gone and gaining it again may never happen. It is far better to never damage it. Think of your family as a fragile growing flower.

Make sure your spouse knows the following: Hit me—I'm gone. Hit our child—you're gone (5–15 years of prison in most states). From the day of your first date, you must let it be known loud and clear that you have a zero-tolerance policy for hitting because violence always escalates.

Children need to see parents protect and honor one another. The days of harsh punishment are long gone, and any parent who can't discipline without resorting to physical violence needs to take a parenting class.

We've all seen it—usually with parents who really shouldn't be—when parents say, "I told you to stop hitting your sister!" followed by a loud slap. What is your child to learn from this besides confusion? They quickly learn they can't trust you, don't like you, and never want to grow up to emulate you in any way. Another thing they may pick up on from such behavior is that it is okay to hit if you are bigger, the one in charge, or a grown-up. It's not a stretch to see what a bad concept this is to foster. You may as well hand them a primer on how to become a bully.

Children do what they see, so make sure they see love and affection in everything you do. Always use "please" and "thank you." Compliment them in front of others, but instruct one-on-one if it is ever something that could be embarrassing. This includes teaching math problems in front of their siblings.

needs

Children have different needs at different times, and it is up to you to notice them. As soon as a daughter approaches puberty, get to the store for a training bra. Nothing is worse for a girl than to have a parent not notice her needs or to put her off until every boy in school is teasing her. You can know each child well enough to sense their individual needs before they do if you care enough to learn who they are inside themselves.

One good way to stay on top of things is to have a weekly family time an hour or so before bed the same day of each week. This is a time when all family members are present—no exceptions. Even if work or school takes someone out of town, they can join in via Skype or the telephone for a few crucial minutes. Have a song, prayer, and spiritual thought if possible. Include the youngest children. Make sure they know they are an important part of the family too. Discuss the family calendar, so you will know what is coming up and won't be surprised to find you need to make cupcakes for seventy scouts at the last minute.

teach

Every moment is a teaching moment. If you lift them up, say, "up." Push them in the stroller and let them point the way. They are thrilled to have the control of turning you left or right. Be sure to speak it aloud for them. "Oh, Mary wants to turn left, so we are turning left now." Let them point with a "magic" wand for even more fun.

Teach small things like how to keep a drinking glass above your meal plate rather than at the edge of the table. This will save gallons of milk, smoldering tempers, and feelings of guilt over the starving children who could have had what was spilled. (Skip that one, please; children feel more than enough guilt from their own minds.) Instructions on how many squares of toilet tissue to use, how to wipe from front to back, and how to wad it up rather than fold it for greater coverage and efficiency are also useful to the child, and can save many an overflowing toilet. Be sure to teach *each* child. You are the parent, and siblings have other plans. You can't expect the trickle-down effect to teach your younger ones.

In the greeting card aisle, I once watched a woman continually scream at her eleven-month-old for pulling out and dropping cards. She wasn't even aware he was trying to model her behavior. I showed her how to point the cart in a way where the baby couldn't reach the cards (safely strapped in, of course) and be given a toy to keep him occupied so she could shop. This simple act saves loads of frustration (. . . and broken jelly jars in the food aisles). Always be prepared by rotating "new" toys wherever you go. By new, I mean something he hasn't seen for a while. Always connect it to the cart so when he drops or throws it, you can easily collect it, and it stays clean.

Be aware a child can't understand the word "don't" because it is a negative concept. Most don't get negatives until they are four or five years old, which is why you will see a mom turning blue yelling, "Don't run in the street!" unaware that to her child, she seems to be saying, "Run in the street!" They simply cannot understand "don't"! Instead, try, "We always stay on the sidewalk," or "Always take a grown-up's hand when you need to cross the street." These sentences are positive concepts their rational minds can grasp. Abstract reasoning takes many years to learn and conceptualize.

enjoy

Nearly any disaster can be overcome if you can find the funny side. Have you ever heard anyone brag about a time they "lost it" with their children? I came into the kitchen one day to find my twenty-month and three-year-old sons thoroughly delighted with the waterfall they were making from the refrigerator ice and water dispenser onto a Hot Wheels track. I smiled and joined them because there was already a floor full of water and crushed "icebergs." What else can you do but enjoy it?

We floated Lego boats, and drove the little cars through it. Later, they helped me clean up and listened when I explained why we'd better not do it anymore. They never did it again, but enjoyed telling their father what fun it had been, because it never became a traumatic event in their lives . . . and that's a good thing.

A recent study called "the Flourishing Families Project" completed five years of a two-state study of some seven hundred families from all walks of life to find out what works for them. Led by Randal D. Day, a professor at Brigham Young University, researchers learned there are happier families than are currently portrayed in popular culture, and "simple things" help keep them together, focused on each other, and confident in themselves.

Kindness, commitment, a willingness to sacrifice for the well-being of the family, and freely forgiving each other were paramount. Families who determined never to talk bad about other family members and to never dismiss another's feelings did better as a family. The "silent treatment" was something never used either. Emphasis on "building" rather than "tearing down" achieved the greatest success. Tradition was important, and things like family meals, prayer, vacations, and celebrations built unity as long as they didn't become routine. Inter-generational ties were meaningful, and children reported good learning experiences from their grandparents.

Keeping distances shorter through social networking sites was something the younger family members particularly liked. Learning that a cousin on the other side of the country was having similar problems at school was helpful to one young participant. Girls, the study found, could benefit greatly from playing video games with their parents. This study is ongoing and will undoubtedly continue to bring to light good information on what brings us together rather than the usual focus of studies on what tears us apart.

Congratulations on your new journey into parenthood. Family life can be fabulous if you learn to find joy in it. One day you will look back and see how fast it flew by. Enjoy every day, every skinned knee, every hug . . . and remember, if you choose a name that doesn't fit, that your child doesn't like, or that suddenly becomes a derogatory slang term, you can always change it.

about the author

KJIRSTIN YOUNGBERG HAS been a photojournalist and author for many years, after selling her first photograph at the tender age of fourteen, and thinking that it sure beat babysitting. She currently enjoys living in a rural farming community with her husband while writing and waiting for her four children to marry and have grandchildren for her to spoil. Two down, two to go, and two grandsons so far.

Linnhe Dhu Images